Hunting ... In Alaska!

Book One

Prepare Yourself
To Hunt "The Last Frontier"

Marc Taylor

www.huntinghardinalaska.com

Hunting Hard...In Alaska!
Prepare Yourself
To Hunt "The Last Frontier"

By Marc Taylor

Published by
Hunting Hard – Alaska Adventures
P.O. Box 233382
Anchorage, AK 99523-3382
www.huntinghardinalaska.com

Published March, 2003
Printed in the United States of America
By Thomson-Shore Book Manufacturers
Dexter, MI

ISBN 0-9726668-0-X

Library of Congress Control Number: 2002116916

Edited in part by Larry Kaniut

Cover Design by Foster & Foster, Inc.
Fairfield, IA

Dedication

I dedicate this work to my uncle, Robert Ross, who lived his life as a simple and mentally "retarded" man, near the tiny crossroads called Williamsville, Mississippi.

My Uncle Rob never drove a car or owned anything of any value. He always carried a pocket full of change, though, in case he got the opportunity to buy someone a candy bar or a soda. With those coins, he *was* rich.

Uncle Rob never had an interest in books other than the bible, as the patience to stimulate a simple man to read had not evolved in the time that he lived his life. I doubt that he ever traveled outside of central Mississippi either, and yet he considered himself worldly because he experienced the many miles that passed beneath his simple feet. You see, my Uncle Rob liked to walk. He walked because he loved to make conversation with the many people who would offer him a ride to his destination.

It must have been nice to see the world through his eyes.

Not many people were fortunate enough to know or appreciate my Uncle Rob, but now - as his name is written on this page, his memory... *is* well traveled; and his name... *is* familiar, if only for a brief moment, to the many thousands who will read this book for the years to come!

Do me the favor of reading these next words out loud, so that his name will have crossed the lips of thousands who did not even know of him...

"You have touched me also, Robert Ross."

Hunting Hard...In Alaska!

Hunting, from the Northwest to Alaska

By Larry Kaniut

Growing up in the Pacific Northwest, I hunted upland game birds and waterfowl with a shotgun; I pursued deer and elk with rifle and archery tackle. The grain fields, sagebrush country and timbered thickets laid the groundwork for my hunting Alaska's really BIG game.

While hunting the Great Land I've been privileged to harvest black bear, caribou, moose, mountain goat, Dall sheep and Old Yellow Eyes.

Within 15 driving minutes of my home, nestled in the foothills of the Chugach Mountains, my wife Pam and I see Dall sheep, bald eagles and beluga whales...moose and an occasional black bear visit our yard in Anchorage.

Alaska is like no other hunting venue. It is twice the size of Texas. Whereas a hunter in the Lower 48 states can hunt a rugged area a few miles square, that area is multiplied hundreds of times over in Alaska. You can fly for hours in a jetliner over snow covered mountains, glaciers and silty rivers. Below lurk swamp bogs, muscle busting ridges, acres of Devil's club, miles of alder tangles, innumerable crevasses, near freezing waters and quicksand-like mudflats.

The 48-state hunter has telephone lines, power easements, roads, fences and human dwellings to call upon for direction or succor. Not so in Alaska. In 37 years of hunting the Last Frontier I don't recall ever seeing a fence in the wild.

There are less than a million people plunked down into a handful of cities and numerous towns and villages in this vast country—nearly a third of the human population lives in

Anchorage. Less than a dozen highways connect Alaska's major population centers, amounting to roughly 3,000 total miles of highway. When you leave the roadside in Alaska, you are in wilderness where danger lurks on every side...be it mountains, glaciers, rivers, wild animals or weather—they'll eat you alive if you are not prepared.

I am no stranger to Alaska's danger filled playground.

When I shot my first moose August 20, 1970, little did I realize that I was experiencing the beginning stages of hypothermia. Nor did I know when I shot my first goat on September 20, 1970, that my friend Lynn Roumagoux and I would spend the night on a rainy mountain in a life or death event. In the summer of 1979 my fellow crew members and I experienced 5 near fatal accidents while commercial fishing the Naknek-Kvichak region in Bristol Bay. My first grizzly was another story. Viewing his eyes reflected in the light of our flashlight from 10 yards was less than comforting.

These early adventures paved the way and filled my mental "danger" journal of things to consider and avoid on future outings. They also enabled me to suggest safe travel in Alaska's great outdoors while compiling 6 survival-adventure books since 1975. Perhaps the introduction to *Danger Stalks the Land* describes Alaska's dangers best:

> Call me danger. Call me death. Call me rugged terrain, hypothermia or severe turbulence. Call me anything you want. But know this. I seek to kill. To maim. To destroy.
>
> I stalk the careless. I lay in wait for the unprepared. I look for the ignorant. I waylay the unsuspecting. I devour the weak. I pursue the complacent. And I embody death.

I go by many names and I'm clothed in many forms. Some of these are avalanche, ice, drowning, mid-air collision, crevasse, freezing, steep terrain, grizzly.

The bottom line is this...if I find you, death follows in my footsteps because...I inhabit the Land of Death.

It was my privilege to meet Marc Taylor at Anchorage's Great Alaska Sportsman Show in April 2001. I would never have thought at that time that he would write a book about hunting and ask me to participate in it. In August 2001 Marc gave me some Dall sheep meat; in September some moose meat; and in October some goat meat—very generous gestures from a new friend (no Alaskan gives away hard won sheep meat!). In like manner Marc shares his knowledge of hunting and shooting.

The information that Marc has put together in *Hunting Hard...in Alaska!* is extremely helpful and should enable any Alaskan hunter, new or veteran, to benefit from his experience.

Larry Kaniut

Larry Kaniut is an accomplished author, a seasoned veteran of the Alaska bush, and a great mentor. I was delighted to have him as a sounding board during the preparation of this book, but will retire him at his request... – Marc

Hunting Alaska Progressively

Chances are that small game animals like squirrels, rabbits, and birds were the first creatures that you sought as a young, burgeoning big-game hunter. I specifically remember my first invitation to go hunting. My Uncle Barney asked that I join him in the swamps and islands of Southern Louisiana. I was the ultimate "city boy", possessing no knowledge of the outdoors or the creatures that lurked there. The single-shot .410 gauge shotgun that my uncle purchased for me felt huge in my young hands, and I was an uncontrollable flincher; which caused me to miss the first of the many rabbits that we saw on my "opening day". It wasn't long though, before I was a successful solo squirrel hunter, and having cured my flinching problem, I had taken my first white-tailed deer by the age of fifteen.

I feel blessed that my first lessons were simple, allowing me to experience and appreciate even the smallest of game animals as gifts. I sometimes cringe when I hear of a very young hunter taking large game animals at an early age, as I hope he has been afforded the opportunity to learn the invaluable lessons of life and death progressively, as I had.

Many years later I found myself fortunate and experienced enough to take on the challenges that are offered by the great land that we know as Alaska. As you will read, I chose to start my Alaska hunting career in the pursuit of caribou of the Mulchatna herd. Caribou are not exactly the smallest game animal in the great state, just the least sophisticated to hunt, as they travel in herds that can number in the thousands.

As you are considering the opportunities available to you by choosing Alaska as a hunting destination, don't succumb to the pressures that would cause you to "bite off more than you can chew" in your first outing. It will be incredibly hard to talk yourself into a caribou hunt once you have taken your first Dall sheep; in the same manner that a youngster loses interest in squirrels and rabbits once the hounds have pushed a white-tailed buck by his stand.

Take the time to appreciate all of the game animals that Alaska has to offer in a progressive manner; you will be rewarded every time that a friend admires your massive caribou antlers, and that alone will drive your desire to return to Alaska in pursuit of increasingly more challenging game animals.

I.
Stories
To Get The
Heart Pumping

"Mulchatna Mardi Gras"

"The Not-so-Solo Sheep Hunt"

"Weyerhaeuser"

"The Thirty-Hour Goat"

"Mulchatna Mardi Gras"

Don't you love getting a phone call from an old hunting buddy? I remember a particular August day in Kansas, when I received one of those calls. He asked how I'd been, and if I'd like to occupy the final spot on a caribou hunt the following year in Alaska. (Wow!) Needless to say I hesitated, for about two beats of my heart, before answering, "Book it, I'm in!" I was pretty modestly employed at the time, but did not have time to figure out the financial part right then. You see, we are afforded very little time to make important decisions in this lifetime, but fortunately we are afforded the rest of out lives to pay off those hastily made decisions.

I had read James Michener's novel, "Alaska", and Larry Kaniut's "Alaska Bear Tales", twice each, in years before, lighting the spark in me to someday rediscover the "Last Frontier" for myself. For the remainder of my life since then I had been totally fascinated with the destination we call Alaska. Unless you get that magical invitation, it's hard to just "up and go", as it seems to be a world away. What followed that welcomed phone call was the slowest thirteen months that I can remember, but before you know it, my wife was sending me off after a few cocktails at the airport outside of Kansas City.

I was traveling to Anchorage through Minneapolis, which is where I would join the rest of the hunting party: Darin Brincks, Dan Niedert, Dirk Sterner, and Scott Destival. They arrived from Waterloo, Iowa, a place that I had called home years earlier. On a connecting flight we traveled to Anchorage, arriving in mid-evening on the 30th of August 1999. We arranged a couple of overnighters before flying on to Aniak, Alaska, where *Aniak Air Guides* would meet us. Spending an extra night or two in Anchorage is always a great idea in the event that luggage is late to your destination. After all, this is your "dream hunt", so why have it end in a nightmare if you can plan otherwise, right? The precautions were unwarranted on this occasion, as our luggage arrived with us, so we used the lag time to do some shopping and fishing.

Aniak, Alaska is located west of the Alaska Range, on the northern shore of the Kuskokwim River. This river is a major artery to the village of Aniak, so everything that is there or has been there has arrived by air or river because of its remote location.

The small airport was bustling with hunters old and new, each desiring a special trophy moose or caribou that would fulfill the soul's yearning for adventure. Only an Alaska hunt can satisfy this certain yearning.

We loaded our gear into a truck for the short ride to the lodge of *Aniak Air Guides*, where we were checked for proper legal hunting documentation and briefed on the legalities of hunting in game management unit 19A. This was my first hunt of any kind using a flight service to reach my destination, so I was very impressed with the thoroughness of the outfit we had chosen. Horror stories abound about unprofessional guides and flight services that put the hunter in jeopardy by putting them into the Alaska bush improperly briefed on the legalities or otherwise of a particular hunting area. If the professionals are not asking questions of you, then you had better be asking questions of your own.

We were thrilled to finally arrive at our destination. With two harvest permits each for caribou in hand, and final adjustments to our gear, we were prepared for our flight by bush plane to our hunting site. I volunteered to be the first person inserted, as I have longed to be alone in the Alaska backcountry. We would be ferried out in turn. Dan and I went in the first two flights by "Super Cub", and the remaining hunters in our party, Darin, Dirk, and Scott came later in the day by "Beaver".

A "Super Cub" is a relatively small aircraft capable of carrying one hunter and gear, plus the pilot. This is the work horse of the Alaska bush planes, due to its ability to maneuver in tight places, requiring minimal take-off and landing area. If you have the feeling in an airliner that you are not actually flying because of its comforts and size, you won't get that feeling in a "Super Cub". This is flying at its most interactive.

A "Beaver" is a bit larger, having a payload capacity of 1200 pounds. That means four hunters, their gear, and a pilot, with room to spare. If a "Super Cub" is likened to a sports car, then a "Beaver" is likened to a pick-up truck. Load capacity and extended range are trademarks of this freighter, which may be second only to the "Super Cub" in the total number of take-offs and landings in the lakes and on the tundra of Alaska.

Both airplanes can be fitted with tundra tires, floats, or skis, depending on the environment and time of year that the flying is done in. I recommend reading about some of the legendary pilots throughout the history of the settlement of Alaska.   It is fascinating reading at best, and will make you look upon the pilot that delivers you to your hunting destination with a sense of awe normally reserved for war heroes.

My pilot and I lifted from the Kuskokwim River in mid-afternoon on the 1st of September. We flew south down the Aniak River; a breathtaking flight over riparian habitat containing bears, moose and the migrating caribou that would occupy all of our thoughts over the next nine days or so. This was truly a religious experience for me, and I was certain it would be only the beginning of a long-lived hunting career in Alaska.

We landed an hour or so later, in a small lake that had been dammed by beavers. I scrambled my gear up a shallow bank in search of a suitable campsite for our party for the following week. I distinctly remember the departing plane lifting off the lake, leaving me behind, alone. Only then did I realize just how alone a person could get in such a huge place. I guess I could have had a concerned feeling, but I didn't. Instead it was a feeling of awe at the vastness of the area around me, with no sign of man's presence to be found. One can easily imagine this environment being the same today as it has been for thousands and millions of years...Wow!

On the flight in, we had seen sporadic caribou in the area of our beaver lake, and the ground was webbed with trails that resemble cattle paths. A rain cloud approached rapidly, so I assembled our dome tent hurriedly. I had heard that the weather up here is unpredictable, at best, so I erected shelter in the flattest place I could find.

Now let me tell you a little about this so called "flat place" that I had selected. It contained what I'll refer to as "tussocks" of dense grass that grow very close together. They range from eight inches to eighteen inches in height. You cannot walk *on* them, because their root system sticks above ground making them very unstable. You cannot walk around them because they grow very close together, pretty much just as wide as your foot. You're left with a combination of *on* and around, which makes for very difficult travel...or sleep. I'm still affirming that this spot was the best that I could find, and I'm still being blamed by my buddies for back problems caused by the uncomfortable sleeping arrangements. The best part is yet unmentioned, though; numerous caribou trails cut right through out camp!

My hunting buddies arrived over the next couple of hours with the same expression on their faces that I had. I'm telling you, we were in the middle of nowhere, Alaska. We make ourselves at home and began to glass for caribou. In Alaska, you cannot fly and hunt on the same day in most cases, so we were restricted to looking and planning only until the following morning. There was a sharp rise in the terrain behind our camp, so I went up for a better look around. I didn't have to travel far to see caribou, which gave me a comfortable feeling about how this hunt was going to turn out. After finding a nice "shed" antler, I headed back to camp for some dinner and rest, which I would surely need in order to pack a caribou in this unforgiving terrain.

We awoke to a welcomed light frost. This would be our insurance against mosquitoes, which had not been bothersome thus far. I had read that the first week in September was the best time to hunt because the mosquitoes had likely been put down by "ole Jack Frost" for the winter. It's nice to hunt without being the hunted, so we got to it.

After a light breakfast of oatmeal, Darin and I paired up and moved off to the west in search of the caribou of our dreams. We really had no destination in mind so we meandered to the southwest on caribou trails until we could see a great deal of country.

Dirk and Scott stuck closer to the lake in moving around it, then split up upon reaching the gently rolling terrain that dominated to the south of camp. Dan hunted the high ground above our camp, as it provided suitable cover. He needed a closer shot, being a die-hard bow hunter.

We were maybe a mile from camp when we decided to stop and glass for a long while. Dirk had been visible to our east, but a great distance away. There were some caribou on the skyline just above him, two of which appeared to be "shooters". We watched as they moved in our direction, and then a shot rang out. Dirk had taken the first caribou on this hunt, only an hour and a half into the first day!

The remaining bull made a hasty retreat...unfortunately for him, he made it in our direction. It took him almost five minutes to cover the ground between us, so I had time to set up a shooting position using my pack. Darin graciously urged me to shoot first, and he would back me up if necessary. I had plenty of time to study the antlers of this bull, which were very palmated at the top of his thick main beams. He was in full velvet, and had not begun to shed.

I allowed him to approach to within one hundred yards before I felt the crisp "break" of the trigger on my .270 *Model 700*. The bull buckled and died instantly. A huge sense of accomplishment washed over me, as I had successfully hunted and acquired a regal Mulchatna barren ground caribou from the tundra of Alaska!

I began skinning and quartering my bull while Darin continued to hunt. It wasn't long before his rifle cracked. I looked up in time to see about a dozen caribou scatter. He had taken a very nice bull about a quarter of a mile closer to the lake than mine. Full velvet was definitely the thing to wear around here, or so it seemed, as the tall antlers of Darin's bull also had not begun to peel.

We had produced four caribou on the first hunting day, as Scott had taken a bull farther to the east. A meat cache was established on the opposite side of the lake from our camp, and we dined on caribou tenderloin that evening. Dan, the lone bow hunter, was above camp on the high ground and had witnessed most of the action. He had seen lots of game, but they didn't provide any shooting opportunities.

The next morning was spent taking care of the meat cache. The weather had turned to a full drizzle, and the temperature hovered at fifty degrees or so. Each meat bag was placed on a bed of willow branches to ventilate the underside. We spread black pepper over the bags to help keep any flies away, then built a shelter to protect the meat from the sun and rain. It would be seven full days before we would be picked up, so ventilating and keeping the meat dry and cool would be very crucial to keeping it from spoiling.

Darin, being a world-class taxidermist began to flesh and preserve the capes. He felt duty-bound, even on his vacation/caribou hunt, and the rest of us were, and still are, in his debt. Late in the afternoon, Dan and I headed for the higher ground behind camp to see what might be stirring...of course I took my rifle, and my "hunting" part of this trip would soon come to an end.

We had not been gone long, nor had we climbed very high when we spotted a great looking herd of caribou in a saddle between two hills, maybe a mile distant. You see, a *great looking herd,* as opposed to just your *average looking herd*, contains a majority of bulls, some of which must be considered exceptional. This is a hunters' definition, of course, and on my second day of hunting we were becoming spoiled by the quantity and quality of game we were seeing.

Taking turns with my pair of *Steiner* binoculars, we decided that they were impressive enough to attempt to get ahead of them, this being a near-impossible feet if caribou are in "migration gear". I had my eye on a particular bull that had begun to shed his velvet. He had long, branching tines at the top of his antlers, and was silver-gray from his shoulders to his head. No sense getting two caribou with similar attributes when you've got this many trophies to look over, now is there? I had been, and am still spoiled rotten by this hunt.

The herd paused in a depression in the rolling tundra, to graze on the lush caribou moss, called lichen (li-ken). It's as if it were meant to be...

Dan stayed put while I did a wide, sweeping, stalk-trot to get ahead of them. This took me to the far side of the closest hill, giving me a broadside view of part of the herd. I guessed them to be at a distance of three hundred yards or so. I shed my rain parka and crawled on all fours, to get a better angle for my shot. I could not see the bull that I mentioned earlier, but there were others, equally as impressive within range if he did not present himself.

My first barren-ground bull caribou.

I was laying flat on my stomach, with the fore-end of my rifle rested on my balled fist; my sling tightly clenched to provide support. It looked as if I would not be afforded a chance to improve my position without spooking the caribou, so I gathered my focus. I waited for what seemed like an eternity before the velvet-shedding bull stepped into my line of sight. ("Click", the safety slid forward.) Through my *Leupold* scope I could see that the velvet was hanging from his antlers like torn rags, exposing bright pink antler underneath.

I concentrated on his right shoulder as he turned and stepped up onto a rise in the ground to face the herd. That's when it happened... my shoulder jerked as the rifle fired. The bull stood with his legs wide apart, fighting the urge to collapse. I cycled the bolt rapidly and touched off another shot in case the first did not find the proper mark. The second shot anchored him to the tundra. The remainder of the herd scattered, and Dan was unable to manage a clean shot on any of the fleeing bulls.

I paced the distance to the fallen bull; about 275 yards. Both shots went in just behind the right shoulder, not very far apart. I stood over my bull, watching Dan approach, when it hit me...my hunt was over. Dan took the obligatory photos of the impressive animal, and then we opened him to allow the cooling to begin. It was near dark, so I would return the next day to quarter and bag the meat.

Upon our return to camp, I was torn between elation and regret for having "tagged out" so early. I remember thinking; hunters that wait too long to fill their tags sometime have to wait until next season, so I traded all regret for the feeling of having accomplished what I had come all this way to do.

On our third day I arose to the dreaded chore of packing my caribou in from the hills. He was nearly a full mile away, and it would take me at least four to five trips. As long as I stored the meat properly, I could take my time in packing it back to camp, I guess. We wouldn't be going anywhere for at least six more days, so I paced myself.

During one of my returning trips I had the pleasure of watching Dan and Darin stalk a herd of caribou on all fours. This took place through my binoculars at a distance of about a mile and a half, on the other side of the lake from our camp. Dan had recently traded the archery equipment for a borrowed .300 *Win. Mag.*, and they both scored on the fourth day. Dan with two bulls and Darin with his second. Scott downed his second bull, also.

From my elevated position above the camp, I watched it all unfold. The first of Dan's bulls staggered a ways and tripped over the meat bags from Dirk's second bull, falling dead... so much for dying with dignity.

At some point during the fracas, a large grizzly bear moved in due to the overwhelming smell of meat and blood in the area. Scott and Dirk were packing meat in the area of the bear's interest, so I began to hurl profanities at the bear in an attempt to alert our unknowing buddies. We watched from camp as the huge bear approached the lake with caution, only to get a whiff of someone's hip waders that had been conveniently stashed near the lake. Once he caught the smell he bolted, and it seemed he would run until he left the county. (There are no counties in Alaska) He had probably been hunted before, and no doubt, would have been a fine incidental trophy had a member of our hunting party been a resident of Alaska.

*I was more than happy to end my hunt with
the taking of this excellent bull.*

When the smoke cleared, everyone headed back to camp to
rehash the day's many events. We were having a grand time
when we spotted a major herd of caribou coming over the horizon.
A *major herd* is one in which the caribou are too numerous to be
counted. This was the single most impressive event of the entire
trip thus far...what seemed to be the entire Mulchatna caribou
herd was about to parade through our camp as if this were a
Mardi Gras parade down Canal Street, in New Orleans.

We could do little but watch with our mouths agape. There was not an unlocked caribou tag in the camp. Dan, who had given up archery in favor of gunpowder in order to be afforded a shot, watched as they came to within rock-throwing distance. We were fortunate enough to capture this all on videotape, however, even without it I could never forget the feeling of how small and insignificant we were next to the migration of this tremendous herd of animals. They numbered in the thousands, and if a person ever views this spectacle firsthand, that person, from then, realizes that *it* is not just about *us*, as humans.

The remaining days of the trip passed slowly, and for the most part, uneventfully. We waited for four sunny days; struggling to keep the meat cool. Hardly a caribou was spotted after the "parade".

The streets of this place had been rolled up just like the day after Mardi Gras, the party being over, and everyone forced to return to their lives until next year.

My life was changed forever on this trip. I returned to Kansas with a resolve to become a permanent part of what I had experienced in Alaska...

Keep reading.

*The Super Cub of "Aniak Air Guides" was heavily
laden with antlers and meat as we began our
shuttled departure from the tundra of western Alaska.*

"The 'Not-so' Solo Sheep Hunt"

I stood eagerly at the counter of the Alaska Department of Fish and Game in mid-town Anchorage. This would be the first year that I was eligible to hunt the coveted Dall sheep as a resident of the great state of Alaska, and I had anticipated the day when I would purchase my first sheep harvest permit. I filled out the required information and reached for my wallet to pay for the permit. The attendant stopped me in mid-reach and informed me that as a resident it's not necessary to pay for a permit to hunt Dall sheep – they're free! Wow, what a great place to live.

Even before my relocation to Alaska in the spring of 2000, I had often dreamed of some day hunting Dall sheep, and had done some internet research to find what the cost of such an endeavor might be. You see, a non-resident must be accompanied by a licensed guide in order to hunt sheep, mountain goats, and brown bear unless you happen to be the first degree of kindred to an Alaska resident. The cost for the services was astronomical, with fees reaching as high as twelve thousand dollars in some trophy areas.

After living here for a year I was now eligible to do it myself, so to speak, and since my hunting buddies were not available due to commitments at work, I would have to go "solo". I was soon to find out that "solo" does not necessarily mean "alone".

I received a tip from a guy at work to get me started. He and I pored over some maps of the Kenai and Talkeetna Mountains, highlighting some areas known to contain sheep. I chose these mountain ranges because of their close proximity to Anchorage, and the fact that they are considered approachable to an inexperienced sheep hunter. Some of the areas he had hunted years before, and some that just plain contained sheep that could be hunted without the use of a flight service. I didn't want to spend a lot of money in my first year, I was just looking for some practical experience in order to become a better sheep hunter later. It's a rare occasion to find someone who will share information about favorite sheep hunting areas, as most experienced, successful hunters in Alaska might let you have a date with the wife, but will not let you have the favorite sheep "honey hole". Being happily married, I was not interested in his wife, so he was forced to release a few sheep hunting locations.

About a month before the start of the season, I talked my wife, Lizeth, into a camping trip. I failed to mention that we would be climbing into sheep country in order to do the camping, but she was sure to mention that I would be carrying the majority of the gear. We called it even and headed south to the Kenai Peninsula. Having parked at a well-used trailhead just off a major highway, we began our ascent up a narrow trail through lush, thick vegetation.

This being July, the mosquitoes were vicious. I broke a limb from a willow and swatted the pests for the gradual climb to a very picturesque alpine lake. There was a slight breeze blowing, keeping the hungry mosquitoes at bay for the time being, so we did some glassing into the mountains on either side of the lake. It did not take long to find sheep, as there were thirty or forty near an ice field to the east and two thousand feet higher than our fourteen hundred fifty foot level.

We planned a course that would take us to within a quarter of a mile of the sheep, but out of their sight. It was a steady climb through and around alder patches--exhausting. There's just no easy way to travel uphill through alders, which have sturdy branches that literally push you backward with each advancing step; unless, of course, you were to bring a chainsaw, which we did not.

My wife was a real trooper through the ordeal. I was so impressed and surprised that she did not demand to turn back. This was really a brutal camping-scouting trip we had going on here, but we did finally reach the intended base camp. I set up my two-person, high-speed-low-drag mountaineering tent while she rested. Hey, only the best gear for a future world-class trophy sheep hunter, right?

We had a terrific view of the sheep above, and a beautiful valley below. The band of sheep was stationary and contained mostly ewes with some adolescent rams. At least there were sheep on the mountain, so I was deciding whether it would be worth a longer trip that would coincide with the start of the season. The ram that traversed the mountain just before dark helped me make that decision. He was very near full-curl, and walked with a slight limp. A loose curl to his horns, probably not something that a seasoned sheep hunter would give a second look to, but to this first-timer he was the stuff that dreams culminated in.

We slept soundly that night to the beat of mosquitoes against our tent. There were so many that it sounded like the constant whine of a distant outboard motor. I truly do not understand how the pioneers of this great state survived in the bush without bug repellent, as the sound alone will drive you mad.

Being resourceful as I am, I decided to leave some of my heavier gear behind when we departed the next day. I would be coming back to this exact spot next month, so I water-proofed my optics, stove, and fuel, and some other non-perishables to be stashed, or "cached", as we call it here in Alaska. This solidified my commitment to pursuing my first Dall sheep in these mountains.

At some time in the following weeks, I took my rifle to the local, state-run firing range to ensure that it was still a "tack-driver"; which it was. I have had this particular rifle for years, a *Remington, Model 700* in *.270 Winchester*. It's fitted with a *McMillan* fiberglass stock and is topped with the best that *Leopold* has to offer. The trigger is set at a crisp two and a half pounds. As a matter of fact, it so impressed one of the range officers, that he inquired as to what I intended to hunt with it.

We both, coincidentally, would be hunting sheep on opening weekend...how about that? He asked where I was planning on going, and like the novice sheep hunter I am, I told him. He took two steps back, scratched his forehead and exclaimed, "Man, you are going to be some tough competition!" Yep, you guessed it; he was heading to the exact same mountain that I had scouted. What a "solo" hunt this was turning out to be. We exchanged names and vowed to signal the other if spotted during the hunt. But that could never happen in the huge state of Alaska, right?

On the eighth of August I drove to my now familiar spot on the Kenai Peninsula. The season would open on the tenth, but I wanted to make sure to establish a base camp, then a spike-camp further into the range to ensure my success. I had used maps to formulate a really solid plan – get above the sheep on the day before season and hunt down to them on opening day. I had been training in the Chugach Mountains, which are mere minutes from my house, so I was confident in my ability to get to where the animals were. My rifle was functioning at full potential, so I felt that if a shot presented itself, I would finally possess one of the finest, most sought-after trophies in North America.

I arrived at my base camp after a climb through the dense alders. It was much more comfortable the second time around. My cache of gear was exactly as I had left it, so I began to make myself at home. I hiked up in light, non-hunting attire, which would remain in my base camp. My clothes were drenched with perspiration, as the weather was incredibly warm, and nothing but high pressure was called for over the next few days.

I glassed toward where I had seen the sheep the month before but they were no longer near the ever-receding ice field, which was now nearly a third the size that it was on my previous trip. Just before dark I spotted movement on the exact same game trail that the limping ram was traveling on – could this be a case of "deja-vu"? I trained my spotting scope toward the moving figure in time to see him – another hunter – walk out of sight near the top of the mountain that I planned to crest on the following day. I was crushed.

The range officer had been right; there would be stiff competition on this particular mountain.

I slept only sporadically that night, disturbed by the image of the hunter above me and gaining altitude. I had come to this spot a full two days early in order to get a head start, and was being bested.

Morning arrived, and I wasted no time in packing my spike camp for the hike to the sheep. I stepped off at maybe ten o'clock and climbed straight up, above my base camp. My hike would take me on a side hill walk with a stream running below me to my right. I would cross a saddle near the ice field, then get on a game trail to take me around a peak of one mountain to a large plateau beyond. This plateau was at an elevation of about thirty-five hundred feet. From there I would hunt from my spike camp.

I arrived after a two-hour climb to find two other tents in the plateau. At this point my confidence was receding faster than the ice field, I think. I was going to have to really hunt smart to achieve my goal of taking a Dall ram this year.

On the evening before the season opened, I glassed down a steep ravine on the southern face of the mountain I planned to hunt. There were sheep bedded halfway down the slopes about fifteen hundred feet below me. I was staring intently at a particular group of sheep when I had that feeling that I was not alone...you know how that goes.

I turned to see someone above me and moving in my direction. The gentleman came to my roost overlooking the ravine and we made conversation about the hunting that would take place over the next couple of days. He mentioned that he had hunted here before with little success, mainly due to the number of hunters present. I felt like I was being crushed like you crush an empty beer can...the possibility that I might not be successful was too much to bear.

Regardless, he was a very pleasant person, and seemed to have a deep respect for the hunt. Of course, he had taken Dall sheep before and possessed an indifference to whether he would pack out a trophy on this hunt. There's quite a bit to be said about the experience you have when you put the pressure of "success" on the back burner, and DeWayne Craig seemed to be having one of those hunts. He offered that it would be better for the situation if we put our tents in the same spot and I had no objection, because I couldn't be in better company on my "solo" hunt. We set up camp out of the way and developed a strategy for the following day.

I got little sleep, of course, in my spike camp next to DeWayne's base camp. I had little more than the rain fly from my tent, a sleeping bag, stove, and a couple of meals. My shelter was propped up by my trekking poles. I am so fortunate that there were no mosquitoes up here, because I had no real protection from them. DeWayne, on the other hand, was from the old school, being in his late fifties or so, and had a deluxe four-man tent. He had little in the way of prepared meals, just some peanuts and crackers.

Each person chooses his load based on personal priorities, I guess. I was comfortable with my Spartan set-up given the fact that we didn't get any rain or high winds during the night. The reason for my inability to sleep was simple – I was in position to harvest a Dall ram, and by morning that would be a possibility. As serious hunters will tell you, so much time is spent in anticipation of the hunt that the last hours before the hunt begins are unbearable. When the sun rises on the tenth of August, a dream long in the making will finally become experience.

And so it happened. The sun's rising, that is... DeWayne and I split up to cover different drainages. I would be a bit farther to the east, both of us hunting the sheep from above. I enjoyed a warm pot of noodles to start the day right, then packed minimal gear for the day's adventures; binoculars, rifle, knife, game bags, a snack, and some water. I loaded three hand-loaded 130 grain *Nosler Ballistic Tip* rounds into my rifle. I chose not to chamber a round for safety's sake. There would be no sense in letting a mishap spoil this little dream I was living.

I covered the ground to my initial glassing position with ease, as it was relatively flat. I glassed down from above and spotted movement almost immediately after first light. Two rams that appeared to be legal crossed the top of a rocky ridge far below me and descended to a small plateau plush with green grass. *This* is when you chamber a round... I followed with my binoculars until they were out of sight. I then descended to gain a better vantage point. The ground beneath my feet was very steep and loose with shale and small rocks. Each step caused a small slide below me, so I was extremely careful about my footing. It is very common to hear and see rocks sliding and tumbling without noticeable reason in sheep country. Therefore, sheep are not easily disturbed by the occasional noise of rocks on other rocks.

I decided on settling into a rock outcropping, maybe three hundred feet under my original position. From here I would wait patiently for the sheep to make the next move.

It wasn't long before a loose band of ewes and young sheep were pushed in my direction from the east. I say pushed, because not far behind were two hunters. They topped a ridge and realized their mistake, but too late. They had skylined themselves and the sheep were watching their every move. Wow, this place was hunted harder than the mountains of Colorado during elk season. To add insult, they were clad in clothing that was entirely too dark! I could spot their smallest of movements from the full half-mile of distance. In Alaska, the only thing that a sheep would see up here that would be as dark would be a wolf or a black bear, and all are predators. I made a mental note to always ensure that my outer clothing is neutral in color, which it was at this time.

Baam! A shot rang out from the west and a bit below me...that may be DeWayne...then a second shot followed. That's usually the sign of a miss, but maybe he had connected with the first. I waited at a higher state of alert, as a wounded or maybe a missed ram may be about to come my way. After an uneventful twenty minutes or so a figure appeared on the skyline to my right. It was DeWayne. I motioned him to my position with hand gestures that included my seeing the two rams below me, so he came slowly to my rock outcropping.

We huddled together and he told me of two nice rams that he had surprised while they were bedded. He took two shots at a distance of about eighty yards or so, but missed cleanly both times. I asked if he had bumped his rifle scope and he said that it was a good possibility because the shots should have found their intended mark. We had no more than winced at the bad luck when we turned and spotted four rams below at a distance of three hundred yards or so. Where did they come from?!

I raised my rifle, as they were already within my comfortable shooting range. My stock was resting perfectly on a flat rock in front of me. Through my scope I could plainly see that the lead ram was a perfect full-curl, which makes him legal.

I asked DeWayne if he thought the same, but he didn't have his optics out. He said something to the effect of, "If you say so, then it's good enough for me."

I kept my crosshair on the lead ram, but they were traveling in such a tight group that he was occasionally overcome by one of the others. I don't remember studying their horns as intently as his, because I was already convinced that he was legal. I kept my focus, and the group stopped, with the lead ram taking two strides forward of the other three.

"Click" went the safety. I had his right shoulder perfectly quartered...the intense concentration took over and...*Baam!* The rifle jerked in my hands. The last picture I had of the lead ram as the shot went off; he was flipping in my scope. That's a good sign, right?

Then the adrenalin took over and I lost my cool. I remember shouting, "Did you see that shot? Did you see him flip?" My new hunting partner was all smiles. "I guess I'm going to help you pack a sheep", he said.

We found my ram piled up, a full-foot off the ground, in the last big bush before a steep drop. He had tumbled more than a hundred yards from the place he and the other three rams were standing. I was more than ecstatic. We did the hand-shaking and back slapping thing, and I reminded DeWayne that he was under no obligation to help me with this sheep. After all, he was on a "solo" hunt as well, wasn't he? He decided to stay and help, so we got to it.

Upon closer examination, the shot on the ram could not have been placed better. He was hit perfectly behind the right shoulder. We estimated the distance to be a little above three hundred yards, downhill, on an angle of about thirty degrees. My rifle is "dead-on" at two hundred yards, so I held point of aim – point of impact. The slope downward would cause a rise in my trajectory almost equal to the drop caused by the extra hundred yards or so greater than my "zero", at two hundred yards. If I lost you, I apologize. It simply means that the time I spent in the Marine Corps as a sniper had paid off in a practical kind of way.

Not long after we arrived at my sheep, two hunters, probably the two that I mentioned earlier, came over to examine our full-curl trophy. Did I mention this mountain was crowded, or what!

This is usually where a hunting story is brought to a close, as to the packing back to the base camp and on to the car would be only sweaty and uneventful. However, this would not be the case on this "solo" hunt.

My greatest friend in the world at this point, and I, loaded our packs equally. He carried a great deal of the meat, and I carried meat, cape, and horns. My load was extremely unwieldy, as all I had for a pack was a canvas day pack. It was one of those left over from WWII, and was effective during the battle at Iwo Jima, but practically useless in my efforts to get my load off this mountain. I had a pack frame at my spike camp, but I would try to make the trip to there with this antique. DeWayne loaded his share into a 1970-something pack with frame that he had tied together with a cotton lashing. What my friend lacked in up-to-date-gear he made up for in brute strength. He was a *packing machine!* Evidently, he had spent much of his adult life in search of adventures; one of which was hiking the *Pacific Crest Trail!* I was out-classed to a large degree; at age thirty-seven, next to this sixty year-old hiking machine.

We took off at a slow pace, as the return climb up the shale and gravel was brutal. Soon we parted ways; each seeking the route that best suits a personal preference for travel. The route to the top that DeWayne had chosen seemed too steep for me, and he was still outrunning me. I had chosen a slight ridge to the east that at least looked a bit less steep, but I doubt that it actually was. We would stop to rest occasionally, he on his ridge, me on mine, except that he was already a great deal higher than I was, and the adventure was about to get more interesting.

I yelled over, "Yep, I guess some people can hike...and some people can shoot!" I got a big charge out of the wit that I had conjured up on such a nasty climb. He didn't hear me the first time so I had to repeat it. I don't think he got it the second time, either, as he reacted by strapping on his pack and charging farther up the mountain.

I was still a good five hundred feet from the top, when, in negotiating a self-made switch-back, I put too much weight on my right leg. My calf muscle, on such a long and steep climb, was stretched to the max. So a portion of it snapped—

Such a beautiful, well planned experience turned ugly very quickly.

I yelled to DeWayne to tell him what had happened. He told me to stay put, that he would return for me after depositing the meat at the top. This angered and terrified me. Here I was on a hunt by myself, and this guy that I had known for only twenty-four hours was going to have to evacuate me, and was already carrying half of my load of meat! I was not going to let this happen, so I got to my feet and hobbled, at a steep uphill angle, using my unloaded rifle for a crutch. I could do it, but not with the entire weight of the pack, so I unloaded the horns and cape to lighten my load. This made the pain bearable, so I *painstakingly* made my way to our spike camp.

Looking back, this happened because I failed to bring sufficient water with me from the spike camp. It was sixty-five degrees and sunny at the top of this mountain, causing me to require more water. I had planned everything, but failed to hydrate properly.

I met DeWayne near the camp; he seemed surprised to see me. I was surprised to see me too, given the pain my leg was in, but I was not going to allow him to spend his hunt nursing me. He had decided to give up the hunt for today as his rifle was not properly functioning, or *something,* so he began packing up his tent and I covered my meat bags with large rocks in a shady spot.

I had chose to travel, with DeWayne, to my base camp, to get a good night's rest, and hydrate. I would return the next day with just a pack frame, water, and lunch, to pack out the meat, cape and horns. I had four days before I was overdue from the hunt, so I decided it could be done, even if it took me a while.

I was covering the meat and DeWayne was packing his camp when we spotted a lone hunter walking across an ice field on the far side of the plateau. Upon glassing him, we found that it was Curt, the range officer I had met weeks before. I motioned him over and proceeded to tell him of our adventures – It's a small world, isn't it? And this IS a crowded mountain.

DeWayne and I packed our gear to my base camp, and then he continued to his car. One heck of a guy this was, and I am forever in his debt.

I went back the next day after a rainy night spent resting in my tent. My leg felt much better, and later I had it explained to me that my calf muscle had created a cast around the torn muscle; protecting it. It was swollen at the time, so it must be true. I normally have "chicken legs" so it was great to see my calf in bodybuilder form, even if it didn't work properly.

Late the following morning I arrived at my cape and horns. The overnight rain had soaked the cape, so it weighed a ton, being full of water. The heat of day had warmed it up considerably, so the flies had swarmed it all morning before I could reach it. All exposed skin had been blown full of larvae by the flies. As a result, I decided to separate the cape from the horns and abandon the cape. I don't entirely regret this as I probably had lost it to the moisture, heat and flies already; had I been healthy, I would probably have a mounted Dall sheep ram in my living room. But to prevent it from being an entire loss, I created a beautiful "European mount" from the horns and skull.

I packed the horns and skull to my meat cache, combined it with the entire quantity of meat, and prepared lunch. This would be one heavy load to pack back to base camp, so I took the time to properly restore my energy and fuel levels before strapping it on.

The entire package, meat and horns probably weighed in the area of ninety-five pounds, so I took it easy on the trip back to base camp. There, I stopped only briefly to rest, then proceeded to my car. For most of the hunt it had been sixty-five degrees and sunny; the meat needed to be stored properly, and soon, so I left my tent and gear in place and would return for it after a couple days of rest and rehabilitation.

I arrived at my house, in Anchorage, at 7:00 p.m. on the 11th of August, worn down from my pack-out with the bum leg and heavy pack. I called DeWayne to let him know that I was home safely.

As you might expect, DeWayne Craig and I became very close friends after this "solo" hunt, and I dedicate this story to him. We have planned a brown bear hunt in the spring, and another Dall sheep hunt next fall. He returned to the mountain a few weeks later to claim his Dall sheep on a truly "solo", single-day hunt, in which all he took was a *new* rifle, and that *rickety* 1970-something pack.

But I'll let him tell that story...

A European mount is an attractive alternative to a full shoulder mount.

Sheep from this area of the Kenai range rarely reach more than full-curl due to extreme hunting pressure.

If you leave your camera in base camp, you'll have to settle for a backyard photo like this one.

"Weyerhaeuser"

Baam! The report from my *.375 H&H Magnum* echoed across the Alaska tundra. The bull moose stood stunned, his amorous intentions brought to a crashing halt by the 300 grain *Partition* bullet just behind the shoulder. I followed with an insurance shot to the upper shoulder to bring a quick passing to this most regal of creatures.

Walking the short distance to this fallen giant, I could feel the beat of my heart in my ears. Nothing gets your blood pumping harder than being in the presence of the largest of the deer species. I had judged him to be nearly sixty inches across the palms of his antlers, and the closer I got the more impressed I was by his massive presence. The trials and tribulations of getting to the bush after the incident on the 11th of September, 2001 seemed so far away now. I had taken my first Alaska bull moose!

This hunt began over two years ago with a solemn vow by three hunting companions, Dan Niedert, Darin Brincks, and myself, to return to Alaska to hunt trophy moose. We had just fulfilled an unbelievable Mulchatna Caribou hunt, and had no idea at that time that I could make the dream of wanting to move to Alaska come true. Well here I am, an Alaska resident, and up they came from Iowa.

Our departure date to the bush on the 12th of September was interrupted by the terrorists' attacks on the day before. All bush planes were grounded along with the commercial airlines. We sat at the air taxi's office all day on the 12th with hopes that the ban would be lifted to allow bush planes to fly. This terrible tragedy had the side effect of stranding scores of Alaska hunters in their campsites on the closing days of their hunts. That must have been something, awaiting pick-up by the air taxi service or guide service that you felt that you could trust, on a beautiful day with not a cloud in the sky, only to realize that there were *no planes at all* in the sky.(?) I read that some "renegades" flew despite the ban, just to drop messages and newspapers to stranded hunters. They did so at the risk of receiving an F-15 escort back to their departure point, as the skies were being closely monitored. Can you imagine getting the news of 9/11 after a week or so in the peaceful Alaska outdoors?

We did manage to get to our hunting destination on the 13th. By the grace of God and the Governor of Alaska...the ban had been lifted!

I had been to this certain area of lakes the year before on a buffalo hunt in which I had a non-resident moose tag. I was taken along by a buffalo permit winner, and would serve as a "pack mule" in the event that we downed a buffalo. We have some of the last free-ranging buffalo in the Americas, so to win a buffalo permit in Alaska requires luck too great to be explained;

this tag is coveted as the most difficult in Alaska to acquire. Here, there are no precedence points; it's truly "luck of the draw".

The buffalo/moose hunt provided me with only a glimpse of a moose that we named "Weyerhaeuser", after the stamp that must have been on the plywood planks appearing to be strapped to his head. We spotted him at a distance of about five miles. He was excavating tundra with his massive antlers to impress a cow moose that had his undivided attention. We tried to call him into range for the next three days, but like I mentioned before, the cow had captured all of his thoughts. To see a moose that is described by my friend, Joe Wilson, a veteran moose hunter, as at least seventy inches and the largest moose he has ever seen; well, that has an effect on a person. The effect being to send you back to the same place at the same time next year to see if you can get a "closer look".

I took my two hunting buddies, Dan and Darin. They hunt hard, as do I, and I knew at least one of us would get another glimpse of "Weyerhaeuser". We arrived at the lakes on the 13th in two *Cessna 206* floatplanes after a breathtaking flight, piloted by two of the more professional pilots in Alaska; Joe D'Amico, and Chandler Wilson. You can contact Jack and Brenda Barber at "Alaska Air Taxi" for one of these flights through the beautiful Alaska Mountain Range north and west of Anchorage.

We started calling for the big boy that evening as we'd seen four big bulls within a couple of miles of the lake during the flight in. Regulations dictate that we can not hunt on the same day that we fly in, so we tried to drum-up some interest for the days to follow.

It was three long hunting days later that I downed my fifty-eight inch moose described earlier. He wasn't "Weyerhaeuser", but I live by the old adage that "one in the hand is worth...", well, you get the idea. Here's exactly how it went:

I had been calling from a spot about four hundred yards from camp for two days. The spot was situated on a slightly elevated, brushy ridge running away from camp to the northeast. I would call at first light for about thirty minutes, then again at dark. The evening of the third day I decided to move about a quarter mile farther away from camp, to the open tundra, but onto a brushy knoll between a ridge and a small pond. I repeated my routine.

It was a cloudless, still, sunny day, and I could hear a twig snap for a mile. The sun now touched the horizon, casting an eerie, golden glow. It's time. My cow calls were echoing in the distance and sounding just as I intended them to...in the manner of, "Urgent, I am the first cow to come in heat this year, and I'll surrender to the first bull that finds his way to this spot. But hurry."

You ever have that feeling that you know things are just right and something is about to happen? Well, it did. The bull started toward me from about a mile or so over the top of a more distant brushy ridge. He was visibly angry, or *something.* He raked every bush between him and me, but still hurried in my direction. I decided to "up the ante" to hurry things even further, so I added a few bull grunts. That did it. He was a mature-antlered bull, in his physical prime, and he was now angry.

Let me tell you, once you have a bull moose decide that he is going to come to your location, with love or fighting on his mind, then you had better be willing and able to down him or turn him in another direction. He will not simply go away disappointed after discovering your presence where there should be a bull and a cow.

The bull was a beautiful, symmetrical sixty inches or so of antler spread; therefore "Weyerhaeuser" would have to wait. It helps to think of the game animal as a gift, and just like at Christmas, we must accept the gifts that are given to us. He was now at a hundred yards and closing fast. I had a small dead spruce that I gripped to steady my aim. Then came the oh-so-familiar concentration that seems to drive your trigger finger... (You see, I used to be a Marine sniper)...*Baam!*

That was the easy part of moose hunting. The hard part being the quartering and hauling, my buddies and I got to it, and had him back near camp by the next evening...a full three quarters of a mile, through the boggiest tundra that a hunter ever had the privilege to hunt. Hey, that's all after the fact, according to my hunting philosophy - Hunt hard!

Now, about "Weyerhaeuser".

We called for two more mornings and evenings from the spot closer to camp before he came in...in all his glory. At exactly an hour and a half before dark, my buddy Dan gave it a fifteen minute session before moving to his overlooking shooting position on a high knoll. Darin and I were now at the other end of the lake trying to drum up some interest.

Dan had no more than settled in when "Weyerhaeuser" approached from the north. There was absolutely no wind, again, so he approached very cautiously, waving his tremendous antlers from side to side for all challengers to see. I think this is about the time you leave the area if you are a lesser bull, but my buddy Dan, being an old "stubborn bull" himself, held his ground.

It takes time to develop the interest of a fine bull moose like the one pictured, which took three days of calling.

"Weyerhaeuser" went to the exact spot that I had been calling from without result, initially. He was about three hundred yards downhill from Dan and made it clear that he was not going to come any closer unless he smelled something familiar, which he did not. I guess that's how you live to reach a ripe old age in the moose world; by trusting only your nose. He got the feeling that there was something wrong with this picture, which there was, and turned to make a hasty exit back to the north.

Dan found a shooting window and touched off a perfect shot, at about two hundred seventy-five yards. (Hey, who's the sniper here? And where did that "lifelong bow-hunter" borrow that rifle anyway?)

The behemoth carried the 180 grain bullet with him about seventy yards before laying down. Dan waited fifteen minutes before moving in his direction. At fifty yards distance the bull locked eyes with the hunter and did everything in his power to eliminate this threat to his domain.

Dan was forced to fire another into him from point-blank range to keep from being run over by the giant bull. The great one died instantly at the second shot. His heart was later found to be pierced by the first slug, and he must have risen on adrenalin alone.

Before we moved him back to camp in nine heavy trips, we measured "Weyerhaeuser's" antlers at 74-½ inches from outside tip to outside tip. This animal will be a sight to behold for many years to come as Dan plans to have him mounted by Darin Brincks, our hunting partner.

Darin and I worked hard for the next four days to try to bring another bull to within shooting range. It just didn't happen. Any remaining bulls must have moved off to celebrate the passing of that big bully, "Weyerhaeuser".

Alaska Air Taxi pulled eleven hundred pounds of meat and three tired hunters out in their flawless transportation efforts. Thanks to them and thanks to the "weather god" for delivering nine of the clearest, least miserable hunting days in Alaska moose hunting history.

Two old bulls and another borrowed rifle.
Dan, after a hunt like this one, it's all downhill for you my friend.
The difference between a really nice bull and a legendary bull
is apparent in the second picture, taken upon return to
Alaska Air Taxi at Lake Hood.

Dan Niedert, the Author, and Darin Brincks

"The Thirty-Hour Mountain Goat"

Goat hunting in Alaska can be one of the most challenging endeavors you can undertake in search of adventure and hunting success. It generally requires months of planning and physical preparation just to put yourself in a position to glimpse one of the most sought after trophies in North America. However, on occasion things come together with such fortune as to make you question the long hikes and endless hours of agonizing over the perfect gear. This is the story of one such hunt.

The "luckiest" part of a trophy goat hunt involves the acquisition of a permit. Depending on the permit area, the usual success rate is between one and four percent. Much like most permit hunts for other species', once a goat permit is drawn, you are only guaranteed access to a geographic location for a specific period of time with the intent of taking the prescribed game animal. That's it. Game density is usually higher in these areas, but in the taking of a mountain goat, there will generally be a great vertical distance between you and your prized trophy.

Let me tell you, vertical distance puts horizontal distance to shame. Here in Alaska, most hikes or pursuits are measured in vertical *and* horizontal miles. Even the most accessible hunting areas will demand that the hunter be in tip-top climbing and hiking shape.

In July of 2001, my buddy, Dan Frost, learned that he had been fortunate enough to be drawn for a mountain goat permit in one of the more vertically challenging areas, but it was accessible from a major highway. Lucky us, right? This would preclude any expensive flights to the hunting area, but it meant that any elevation gain would have to be gained on foot. We both had moose hunts planned for later in the year and so we could only dedicate a three-day weekend to search for a mountain goat.

We planned an entire day to get to the hunting area, where we would set up a base camp; one day of hunting, and one day to get back home in time for work. A seventy-two hour goat hunt? Who is kidding whom, here? Realistically, this would only turn into a three-day brutal camping trip. That is what we thought, but decided that there would be nothing gained if nothing ventured; so we left my driveway at mid-morning on a Saturday.

Our drive to the hunting area was the usual breathtakingly beautiful drive out of Anchorage. I feel truly sorry for the person who does not take in these views of Alaska on at least one occasion in a lifetime. I feel really privileged to live here...

We parked our vehicle off the main road at an unmarked trailhead and started our ascent. In that we would only stay for two nights, we were not heavily laden with gear. All trips into the Alaska wilderness require certain necessities, however, so really the only thing we were lacking was the additional food for a longer trip.

Goat hunting is fueled by calories, so more food than a person would normally require is absolutely essential to sustain the energy necessary to get to the animals' habitat. The usual high-tech "spend-a-lot-of-money-to-cut-down-the-weight" gear has to go along because you have to make it "pay for itself" so to speak.

We climbed up and over the top of the first pass to settle our camp in a level spot. There was a small lake nearby, fed by crystal-clear mountain run-off water. Before us was an additional climb of about a thousand to fifteen hundred feet, over and around an unnamed mountain to put us in a large bowl between two peaks. This is where Dan had previously spotted a small band of mountain goats earlier in the season while scouting from the air. Up here, it's an extra special bonus if you have a friend with an airplane, and Dan has an arrangement with a friend that would be hard to beat and impossible to pay for.

A light drizzle (manageable) soon turned into heavy sleet (miserable). We set up our tent and set about making ourselves at home in this heavenly spot with views of two huge glaciers. If the endeavor fails to turn into a hunt, as can often happen in Alaska, we still managed to camp in one of the more scenic places on the planet. About now I remember us discussing not to continue up to where the goats would be because of the weather system that had recently moved in. The discussion didn't last long as our desire to at least get a look at some goats overcame the discomfort that would certainly be experienced before the day would end.

Dan slung his *Browning .338 Alaskan* across his back. That gesture told me we would be climbing soon – in the sleet – up a pretty steep mountain. To say the least, *I was overcome with joy!*

Our first obstacle was a waterfall that had to be negotiated hand-over-hand. This put us on a large ridge, covered with mountain willows, above our camp.

Mountain willows are knee- to thigh-high bushes with thick lower limb systems. They are specifically designed to entangle the feet and legs of any passers-by. Easily, you can spend too much precious hunting time negotiating your way through mountain willows, but there is no way to avoid this unpleasantness.

We struggled through the thick foliage to a steep slope covered with slick, wet decaying grass called "deer cabbage". I haven't figured out how the name came about, but it is a very slick grass that grows on many slopes. I always travel with a trekking pole, and had to drive it into the mountain at each step to make any progress. Coming down a mountain is always more challenging than going up, so I thought that this particular descent later in the day would surely be memorable.

We had gained over eight hundred feet above camp when I turned to look back at the breathtaking view. The driving sleet obscured the view part, but my breath was taken when I realized how steep our climb had been, and that we may very well be coming down this way later...with a very heavy load.

I remember thinking to myself, " Well, if the hunting gods are smiling today, maybe they won't allow us to take out a goat on this day."

The climbing was slow and steady at this point, with great focus as to proper placing of the feet and hands, which were both getting cold. The terrain flattened out a great deal at about three-quarters of the way to the top, so we traversed to our left until we could see nearly the entire bowl between the peaks. We stopped to adjust our gear and do some glassing through wet binoculars. This is where the story gets good...

Dan was behind and to my left at a distance of about ten yards. He was checking the function-ability of his soaked rifle and removing the water from the scope covers that are supposed to keep the water out. I made a mental note never to get a set of those if we ever make it back to Anchorage – the flip-open kind...

We had about a thirty-mile-per-hour wind at our backs and the sleet was now blowing sideways. I was looking hard at a boulder two hundred yards above and in front of me when two mountain goats jumped up onto the rock! I froze in place, and hoarsely yelled to Dan, "Don't move!" The goats were looking straight through us, and I knew that we had blown it, when they, in turn, jumped off the rock in our direction!

When they were out of sight and below us, Dan crept forward to a large rock outcropping and set up a hasty firing position. The animals were moving to our left, and were below us now, as Dan brought the rifle to his shoulder and began trying to find them in the scope. Dan was directly in front of me at about twenty yards and the goats were directly in front of him at about ninety yards. I could see them over his left shoulder, and it would have made one heck of a picture.

The goats seemed to be twins, as their horns were practically identical. At this point Dan was moving his rifle from one goat to the other trying to find that magical half-inch of extra horn or particular trophy quality that would make one goat stand out over the other. After a moment the goats turned and began to walk toward a cliff and would surely disappear, in seconds – and my hunting buddy was still field-judging them! I almost shouted, "Shoot!" when his *Browning* roared, dropping one of the animals in its tracks. We both threw our arms in the air and shouted with elation!

Goat hunting takes the hunter into beautiful, yet unforgiving country.

After a great deal of back-slapping and hand shaking; him thanking me for spotting the goats, and me riding him for not shooting when *I* had the shot, we moved to check out his downed goat. The 210 grain *partition* bullet anchored the 9-7/8" horned mountain goat, killing it immediately.

This was at 4:15 p.m. on Saturday, the first day of our three-day adventure!

We field dressed the goat where it lay, and decided that it was definitely too dangerous to try to make it back to camp with the goat on such a slick downhill descent, on such a nasty day. If the weather were just as miserable tomorrow, at least we would have the entire day to get the goat off the mountain. Upon agreement that this would be the game plan, we headed toward the slippery slopes and our dry tent somewhere below.

During the trip back we got a scare when Dan lost his footing and began sliding through the grass and low bushes toward a drop-off. He was flailing with both arms, trying to grab something to hold as the ground was rushing by. All I could do was watch...

He managed to grab a thick shrub mere feet from the drop-off. Had he gone just twenty feet further, he would surely have suffered major injuries. If we had packed out the goat, he would have been too heavy to stop, and this story would not be named as it is...

In Alaska, decisions as simple as the one we made not to rush, are usually the fragile difference between life and death.

It rained through the night, and we got little sleep in our dry tent. We simply could not stop rehashing the day's events.

We awoke to a thick fog, but no precipitation was falling. When the fog lifted, it revealed blue skies, so we quickly began our climb back up to the goat. Sunlight and wind had nearly dried the grassy slope, making our trip much less treacherous.

We boned the meat, and kept the entire cape and skull, leaving the bones under a pile of loose rocks.

There was no rush in getting back, so we were careful to keep our feet under us on the way down to camp, which we packed up; just in time for the next deluge of rain and sleet to begin.

I was again joyous at the prospect of walking out to the vehicle

*Hunting during less than favorable conditions
produced this fine trophy goat for Dan Frost.*

with a heavy, rain-soaked pack, but hey, we had what we had
come for and were on our way home on just the second day!

Dan and I arrived back at my home at 4:30 in the afternoon
on Sunday; hence the name of this story. Though far from the
typical Alaska mountain goat hunt, I could not have been more
proud of our accomplishments...unless of course, I had been the
one with the permit!

II.

Steps Toward

A Successful Hunt

Once the decision is made...Don't look Back!

Make a Firm Commitment

This is when the dreams materialize into an eventual reality, and will come in the form of a threshold in time. Maybe a good hunting buddy just planted the seed; or maybe it was something that you read or saw. Regardless, there should be no turning back once you have made the decision to hunt Alaska, as you have just put into perpetual motion a yearning that will cause many restless nights in the passing time between the crossing of that imaginary threshold, and the actual hunting experience. From that moment on, you must proceed with conviction and determination, allowing only the matters that are not within your control to change your plans.

Often the decision to travel to, and hunt in Alaska is made years in advance. In my case, we had thirteen long months to acquire the gear and knowledge necessary to carefully carry out our endeavors, and we proved that such advanced planning can and will make a world of difference in your level of confidence. This will seem hard to believe, but at this moment in time it is not necessary to have any prior information about your hunt except the fact that you have made the commitment to achieve the goal of hunting in Alaska. All other details can be worked out in due time. For instance, say to yourself, "Tom, Dick, Harry, and I will be hunting caribou in Alaska when the season opens in the fall of next year." That, my friends, is the starting place.

Now, having committed yourself and maybe a couple of buddies to such a life altering experience, you must gather necessary information.

Begin to Gather Information

There are numerous sources of information that will aid you in beginning your planning. And, obviously, there are agencies that would love to take your hard-earned money; in exchange, they will provide services to complete, that they can arrange everything except the pulling of the trigger. All you will need in this situation is a valid credit card with a rather large limit. In that case, this book will do you no service; remember this is about doing it yourself from beginning to end. We can now discuss where to look in order to be self-sufficient. I have listed the three sources that I feel will be most useful to the do-it-yourself planner.

Internet

This is by far the most complete source of information, and its use will be vital to your success. By simply searching "Alaska Guides" you will be linked to a wealth of information about the professionals who make it their business to help you get what you are looking for in an Alaska hunt. Also, the "Alaska Department of Fish and Game" has a website that lists all forms of useful information, even down to what gear to bring on your hunt. This site provides the complete hunting regulations for the state, which is broken down into twenty-six *Game Management Units*, each with regulations specific to the unit as well as how your hunting in that unit will be affected by the state regulations. Portions of some sub-units are huntable by drawing only, and applications are available online for the following drawing period.

<u>Word of Mouth</u>

Undoubtedly, you know someone whom has hunted Alaska. If this is the case, invite that person over to have a cup of coffee, or *something*, and allow them to spill useful information to you. Hunters whom have hunted Alaska love to share their experiences, and can lead you easily in the right direction. Often, bad experiences are noted, so be sure to listen for the hard-learned lessons of others in order that you may not have to make the same mistakes. In the case that you do not know someone with first-hand Alaska experience, talk to your local taxidermist; that person undoubtedly can lead you to individuals with the kind of knowledge that you are looking for.

Remember, you will be dealing with other hunters like yourself, and sometimes we tend to exaggerate details a bit. For instance, a hunter may feel that a certain air taxi service or guide service did not put him into an area containing a fair amount of game animals. This may be true, however it could also have happened that the hunter failed to properly prepare himself for the rigors involved in hunting Alaska; and subsequently did not hunt hard enough to see the amount of game he was told would be in the area.

I know of very few professionals, whose livelihood depends on creating a healthy client base, who would put one or a group of hunters into an area where there is no game. This would be too detrimental to the reputation of the guide service to do so. Ask questions of your own and pay careful attention to details that are logistically related. My point is that you must filter out the facts from the judgments in order to reach your own conclusions.

Advertisements

We, as sportsmen, page through numerous hunting magazines in the "off" season as well as the "on" season. Take the time to investigate the ads placed in the magazine by a guide service offering a hunt similar to the one you may be looking for. Fully-guided hunts are expensive, but phone calls are cheap these days; just keep in mind that you will be speaking with a salesperson who wants you to book a hunt with them. Remember to turn on your "filter" when listening to tales of guaranteed hunts at minimum prices. There are no guarantees in Alaska, except that at some time during your hunt, you will be extremely tired, and sore. Ask for references, and check them thoroughly.

The goal, when speaking to references, will be to learn whether the services were delivered just as explained, and don't forget to ask in a respectful manner, "What could the guide service have done to make the hunt an even better experience than it was?" Remember, you are speaking to someone whom you were referred to, so you will not usually hear unsatisfactory comments. If you get referred by the guide or flight service, to someone who had a horrible experience, then you are dealing with a bunch of knuckleheads to start with. Wouldn't you agree?

You may not intend to use the services of a guide, but rather a flight service or air taxi service to put you in the general location of game animals of your choice. Be specific about your requirements when discussing your hunt.

For instance a "drop camp" is when you will be afforded the use of camp equipment that belongs to the flight service. This is extremely convenient as it will reduce bulky gear that would normally make the journey through the maze of airport security; however, this service will add to the cost of your trip. Additionally, the gear you will be using will not be gear that you are comfortable with, nor will you be aware of the true condition of this gear. If it breaks down, the flight service will not be refunding your hunt.

There is a delicate balance between what gear should and should not make the journey; just remember to ask lots of specific questions about what is offered, and what condition the gear will be in when you attempt to use it. Generally, as I have stated before, you will be dealing with professionals who will want repeat business in an increasingly more competitive environment.

If All Else Fails...

Contact me; we'll discuss what's necessary to make you feel comfortable putting your life in the hands of the professional guides and air taxi services throughout Alaska.

Game Management Units

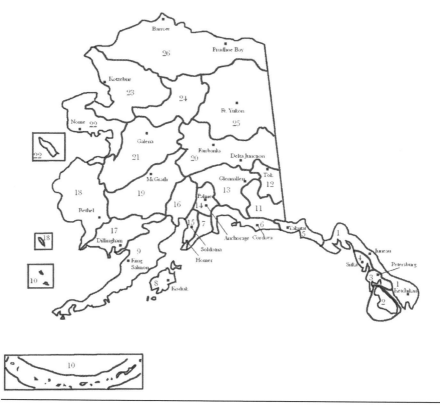

Alaska is divided into 26 Game Management Units, each with regulations specific to that unit.

Long Range Planning

At this point you should have the following basic information in order to begin your planning:

- You have identified the person or persons who will be accompanying you on your trip to Alaska.

- You have identified the species of game animal that you will hunt.

- You have chosen an area of the state or have identified specific Game Management Units that you will target in your search for information.

- You have chosen the dates that you would like to hunt and the duration of your entire trip. These dates will coincide with the season dates of the specific Game Management Unit(s) where you plan to hunt.

*** Always allow *a minimum* of two weeks, door to door, for any hunting trip to Alaska. This will drastically improve your odds for success on any game animal. Additionally, should you fulfill your hunt early; this will allow extra time to arrange for the transport of meat and horns or antlers from the hunt area to your home. The guide or air service will help you plan the adequate duration of your hunt, as there are many factors, including weather, which will effect your actual travel dates. More on these specific factors in following pages.

Reverse Planning

If you have general answers to the preceding points of importance, you may continue to plan your trip by arranging for reservations and accommodations. It is imperative that you plan the specifics that are closest to the hunting area first, as your flight dates to and from your home will be dictated by the dates that you travel to and from the hunting area. I suggest that you arrange the specifics of your trip in the following order:

1. Identify the guide or air service that you will be relying on and the specific dates of your travels to and from the hunting area.

2. Identify the mode and dates of your travel to the guide or air service. This may require airline travel to a destination in addition to your travel to your initial destination of Alaska. For instance, in "Mulchatna Mardi Gras", we established that *Aniak Air Guides* would take us to the hunting area, and that they would do so on or about 1st of August, for a approximately eight days of hunting. This dictated that we should arrange transportation to Aniak, Alaska on the morning of the 1st of August, with a return on the 10th of August. With this information, we planned one day of "down time" before our trip to Aniak, and one more day of down time returning from Aniak. This dictated our airline reservations to and from Anchorage, from our home cities.

3. Arrange for the transportation of your meat and antlers from the hunting area. This may be through an air cargo service. Ask your guide or flight service for the recommended air cargo service that serves your hunting area through Anchorage, if this is your port of entry into the state of Alaska.

4. Arrange your airline travel reservations to and from your home city. Ensure that you are not rushed in case you have connections, as delays happen often, and you will want as much time for you and your gear to overcome those delays and still make it to connecting flights.

5. Arrange hotel stays or other sleeping arrangements as needed during your travels. Ask about the availability of a courtesy shuttle to and from the airport, and make sure that it runs regularly. If there is no courtesy shuttle, you may want to rent a van. *Do not* rent a car. It will not be large enough to accommodate you and your gear.

6. Finally, arrange for the care of your antlers, cape, and meat upon your triumphant arrival home. If you will turn your cape and antlers over to a taxidermist, ensure that they are informed of your return date, and will be expecting your delivery of those items. Notify the meat processing plant that you will be delivering game meat and the approximate date of its arrival.

Don't wait until you are standing in your grossly inadequate living room to make these decisions, as this will be a hard fall from the cloud that you rode home on.

Ask your taxidermist about your holding on to your antlers until your cape has been processed. In this way, you will have your antlers at your home to show to your admirers, not just pictures. This will add tremendously to your overall experience, as it is a drag to return from a successful hunt and not see your antlers again for almost a year while your mount is being processed.

Specifics on Transportation and Accommodations

By using the reverse planning described above, the time period before you actually purchase your ticket will be more flexible, allowing you to shop for rates.

In general, airlines accept bookings up to six months in advance; therefore you may be planning your hunt well in advance of the actual *purchasing* of airline tickets. When looking into flights to Alaska, be aware that the airlines significantly scale down operations during the winter months due to reduced visitor traffic. The number of flights doubles in May, when the hordes descend upon the beautiful tourist destinations, and continue at peak levels into the middle of September.

When those seats start selling, they will sell fast, so you will need to monitor ticket availability far in advance of your actual flight dates in order to purchase a ticket within your prescribed dates and times. This will be especially important to you if trying to fly together with your hunting buddy or buddies.

For the sake of safety, purchase all of the tickets for your trip during one phone conversation to ensure that you will all receive the same rate and sit in adjoining seats. As a lesson, I once tried to purchase similar tickets with phone calls no more than ten minutes apart, and I almost reached through the phone when I was told that the fare had just increased by one hundred dollars!

As far as when to actually make the call, personally, I would purchase tickets five to six months out, regardless of the price. Remember, you have specific dates of arrival and departure to meet, and the time of departure and arrival are more flexible at six months than they will be when booking at three months out. The bottom line is – Don't procrastinate!

Purchase the seat to your dream hunt at your earliest possible convenience and make sure that the tickets are *changeable* in the event that you are held up at an intermediate destination.   Any changes will incur a fee, but you will want to stay on track. Stay away from flying standby as if it had a *plague* bug attached to it. All flights at this time of the year will already be "bulging at the seams".

I suggest that you talk to an agent of the airline that you will be traveling on when booking your flight because you will want to know specific restrictions on baggage (gear) before you arrive at the ticket counter to check in for your flight. After standing in those long lines that we have become accustomed to in airports, you will not be comfortable with moving to the back of the line to repack your gear.

Traveling has become increasingly difficult.   If you are traveling with bulky baggage, as most hunters are, and someone will need to heft your baggage onto a conveyor belt, ensure that they can do this without damaging themselves or your gear. If your gear causes undue mental and physical stress on an individual just trying to do a job, then that person will take out a measure of frustration on your gear when no one is looking.

Be guaranteed of that.   Do not give a non-hunter an opportunity to damage your rifle or bow, thus potentially ruining your hunt, because you were too cheap to purchase the proper traveling case for your most important piece of gear. I own a heavy gauge aluminum travel case, which is virtually impervious to damage by even the roughest baggage handlers, and it sells for less than two hundred dollars. Contact *Cabela's* at 800-237-4444 for a catalog.

Your ultimate goal is to return with meat and memories. Some of those memories will likely be in the shape of antlers or horns, and a cape. The airlines recognize that they are doing business in one of the most desirable hunting destinations. In return, they are willing to work with you in getting your meat and antlers home as long as it is done with no impact to the other passengers. The following is some general information concerning the transport of antlers, game meat, rifle, pack, and excess baggage. This information will of course be time-sensitive, as regulations change with the times, so ask questions and get answers!

Allowable Checked Baggage

In addition to your rifle case, you will be allowed to check two bags or boxes, each of which must not exceed fifty or seventy pounds – depending on the airline. Contact them for details.

Antlers – Antlers must be shipped by air cargo to your destination. This can be arranged through *Alaska Air Cargo*, (800) 225-2752. They will ship to the nearest *Alaska Air Cargo* hub near your home and from there it will be picked up by *Federal Express* for shipment directly to your address of choice. There will be a substantial fee associated with this service, but it is necessary in order to have your memories, in their physical form, sent home. My advice to you is to bring an extra $500.00 or so just for this purpose.

The field preparation prior to shipment will involve putting rubber hose or cardboard on the tips of your antlers to ensure that other cargo is not damaged in shipment. Also, all meat must be removed from the skull plate. This process is not a task to be taken lightly and you must plan to have at least one full day in order to accomplish this task. Contact *Alaska Air Cargo* in advance to learn the details associated with your particular destinations.

Additionally, there are taxidermists who will package and ship your antlers for you for a fee. I will list a few that provide this service in the appendix of this book.

Meat – If you choose to transport some of your meat home with you on the airline, you will be allowed to do so; however, it must be packed to travel, and the airline does not accept responsibility for its spoilage or damage. Your options are to travel with a portable cooler, which you have purchased in Alaska, or to pack it in plastic and waxed boxes, which your guide will provide.

In the case that you are on a do-it-yourself hunt, you may need to purchase boxes of your own. This can be done at any major grocery store in Alaska. In either case, it is a good idea that the meat be partially or wholly frozen upon your arrival at the airport on your way home. This can be accomplished by arranging for your meat to remain in a freezer for at least one overnight stay before continuing your travel. Arrange for this to happen using the air cargo carrier that transports your meat from the hunting area, or the one that will be transporting your antlers and meat to your home.

Dry ice can be purchased before you fly, if necessary, but it must be declared when checking your bags onto a flight. You will be limited to a couple of pounds of dry ice, and there is a limit to the total amount that will be allowed to board the aircraft. Freezing your meat is safer for everyone involved, so arrange some time in a freezer.

Now do you see how important it is to plan extra days to ensure that "what you came for" makes it back home?

Rifle – It must travel with you on the airline, as you cannot send it legally any other way without a tremendous hassle. It must be in a crush-proof case, must be unloaded, and must be declared as a firearm when you check your baggage. A rifle, leaving Alaska with a hunter, may count against your *allowable checked baggage*. This means you may be allowed only one checked bag, plus a rifle case, plus a carry-on bag. Call ahead!

Backpack – Internal or external frame, the best way to get it from point A (Alaska) to point B (your home) is to send it through the *U.S. Postal Service*. I have done this on several occasions, and it practically beats you home. Don't bother with first class postage, as it will only make one day's difference in the time it reaches you, but always, always, insure it for more than the contents are worth. Duct tape it on all surfaces that can be dragged across the ground. I once had a Postal clerk drag my pack out to me when I came to pick it up, and yes, I almost went "postal" on him. The point is - protect your gear. I have had the same hunting backpack for years, and always send it back through the mail. This saves a lot of trouble, and frees up space in your allotment of *allowable baggage* for meat.

About those Accommodations – Expect to pay at least $150.00 (yes, you read that right) per night. This is due to the fact that you'll be traveling through Alaska at the height of tourist season. Of course, as "shooters" we don't consider ourselves tourists, but we are afforded the same accommodations as the business travelers and tourists. I suggest something near the airport in order that you will be near the offices of the air cargo carriers in case you require liaison with them to discuss gear or meat. The area near the airport is buzzing with taxi activity, so you'll nave no trouble finding a ride to shopping or landmark destinations.

Make an advanced reservation at either a full-service or a limited service hotel depending on what you are most comfortable with. Full service hotels offer a restaurant and lounge, but there are many eating establishments within close proximity of all local hotels. If you are seeking to relax and enjoy the out-of-the-way sights of Alaska, consider a "bed-and-breakfast" in or near Anchorage, or your port of entry. You won't be as accessible to shopping and the bustle of Alaska, but you will be nearly guaranteed beautiful sights and a relaxing atmosphere. Oh yeah, and breakfast!

Regardless of the accommodations you choose, it will be evident by the amount of gear you are traveling with that you are a hunter, intent on taking more than just pictures home with you. Present yourself in a well-dressed, respectful manner to everyone you come in contact with. It is of tremendous importance that we, as hunters, are represented in a professional manner at all times in order that we may continue to be accepted worldwide as welcomed guests.

Be attentive to this matter in all aspects of your travel to and from Alaska.

Proper Long Range Planning will help produce long-lasting memories. My buddy Dan Niedert has to look at this mount of Weyerhaeuser for the remainder of his life. The makeover was courtesy of Darin Brincks of Washburn, Iowa.

III.

Gearing Up

Come "loaded for bear". *Kelly Spoonts, of Nikiski, AK was -
on this Spring brown bear hunt in the Alaska Mountain Range, and
this bear still took ten rounds from a Weatherby .338-.378 before
realizing that it should no longer be walking.
Heike Frost and Lisa Bern of Anchorage found their gear more than
adequate to hunt black bears in the Prince William Sound*

Gearing Up
For Success

There is no correlation to the quantity of gear that you bring to Alaska and the amount of success that you will have during your hunt. Further, the improvement of your odds will come from the quality of gear only if your confidence level is increased in proportion with the level of quality of that gear. For instance, a $200.00 spotting scope or rifle, in the hands of a professional, will be more effective than a $1,400.00 spotting scope or rifle in the hands of a 'knucklehead'. With that said, we will begin to discuss some of the traits of gear which will assure that it adds to success. We will not discuss particular models or brand names because we are not equally able to afford the finest *Sako* rifle topped with the finest *Zeis* scope, for instance. If you are on a budget, then you need to purchase the best that your budget will allow for, and make yourself comfortable and confident using that gear.

Let's start with the necessities:

Clothing for Comfort and Utility

The clothing necessary to pull off a successful caribou hunt in August or September is not very different from the clothing necessary to pull off a spring brown bear hunt in the Alaska Range with eight feet of snow on the ground. You will find that hard to believe, but I can assure you that I have hunted both with very close to the same amount of gear. The most important factor is the composition of the clothing and its insulating effectiveness when applied in layers. And weight, of course.

In Alaska, we have a saying, "Cotton Kills". Cotton clothing is heavy, doesn't dry easily, and will effectively pull heat away from your body when damp or wet. I agree with the cotton industry that there is nothing more comfortable than cotton, but that is only the case when it is dry. Because you will either be drenched in perspiration or precipitation while on either a cold- or warm-weather hunt, you must stay away from cotton materials when choosing your hunting clothing. The only cotton that travels with me on a hunt is a thirsty cotton wash towel to wipe perspiration and provide general sanitary functions.

The alternatives are polyester fiber materials, or wool, including fleece. Polyester fibered materials come packaged under a variety of name brands too numerous to mention. What is mentionable about them however is that they are lightweight, don't hold water readily, and dry very easily. Your body will attempt to heat any water trapped next to it, causing you to surrender precious body heat. Result; hypothermia.

Some brand name polyesters are interwoven with elastics that give them a flexible, four-way stretch capability that is important to walking and climbing activities associated with some hunts. I have successfully "walked dry" all of my polyester clothes, once wet, in the everyday rigors of hunting; this would be nearly impossible with any other fabric. Seek these materials and buy them in layers to increase their heat holding qualities.

If you note closely some of the pictures from my hunts, I am wearing polyester shirts and pants that are not even camouflaged, but they are comfortable, even when wet. The fabric is called *Worsterlon*, and is available through *Cabela's*. Remember, we're not hunting white-tailed deer up here, within a couple of miles of a warm vehicle.

If camouflage is necessary or important to you, just make sure that the materials that they are made of are polyester based. No problem, there are tons and tons of those on the market.

Wool is my favorite for it's insulating qualities, and it will hold a great deal of water before you will begin to feel cold, but once wet, wool is nearly impossible to dry without clear, sunny weather. The weight of wet wool clothing can be unbearable on extended hunts in which a lot of ground is covered. On my most recent hunt for Dall sheep, I was wet for five solid days, and in those five days we received less than five minutes of warming sunshine, so don't count on drying days, they are a blessing, but cannot be counted on to dry soaked wool. Take this material only when you can be assured that you will not become soaked in it, and when you will not be packing it out once it is wet.

Footwear for Comfort and Utility

In the discussion of footwear for your Alaska hunt, there are a couple of questions that need to be asked. 1. What is more important to my hunt, comfort or weight? 2. Will fatigue be a factor on my hunt? Once these questions have been answered truthfully, you can begin to choose the boots or shoes that will be right for your adventure. Here are some arguments to consider that will directly affect your level of comfort and fatigue:

If you will be walking long distances and covering vertical as well as horizontal miles, you must consider lightweight footwear with excellent traction. In choosing light weight, you will be sacrificing insulating qualities and maybe water repellency as well, but you will cover more ground with lightweight hiking shoes or boots before becoming tired. After walking through wet grass for most of a day, there is no boot that will be totally waterproof, so your feet are bound to get wet. If I'm going to have wet feet, I would at least like them not to weigh a ton. Insulated boots become extremely heavy once wet, and will be just as cold when you put them on in the morning, so I'll put on a pair of cold, lightweight hiking shoes every time to avoid fatigue plaguing my hunt more than will already be necessary.

However, if I will not be traveling great distances, like on a fly-in moose or caribou hunt for instance, comfort will take the form of insulated, waterproof boots due to the decrease in my activity level. On a hunt such as this, waders will nearly always supplement your primary footwear for travel through the extra wet habitat that most of the Alaska game animals reside in. But not for the alpine critters like sheep and mountain goat, unless you have been instructed to bring waders along.

Plastic boots designed mainly for climbing have become the rage among local sheep and goat hunters. I personally would not recommend them on hiking hunts as they are rather rigid and can dish up a great deal of punishment to the knees. These boots cannot be beat for traction above tree line, however, and all that is left to be said about them is that they have removable liners that will dry more readily than traditional boots. Quite expensive at this writing, the price of plastic boots surely will fall as they become increasingly popular or unpopular.

The most popular boots on the market today are the leather varieties, or a combination of leather and cordura. There is a large disparity between good boots of this variety and excellent boots of this variety, and the often-mentioned saying applies, "you get what you pay for". Most will repel water due to a sewn-in *Gore-Tex* bootie, but not for the life of the boot. With average use, the water-proof barrier will only last for about two years before leaks will develop. Once they become wet, these boots are heavy!

On my most recent sheep hunt, I was wet for the entire trip. I wore a lightweight pair of hiking shoes that did not even claim to be water repellent. I never managed to "walk them dry" but the temperature never got below forty-five degrees, so I was not uncomfortable. I have to stress that you must take the time to dry your feet for at least eight to twelve hours each day in this situation. If you allow your feet to fail due to excessive moisture, your hunt is over and you may find yourself in a survival situation.

Take the time to adjust the laces of your boots often to ensure that your footwear is snug on your feet. This will reduce ankle and foot fatigue, and will ensure that your boots or shoes meld with your feet. In other words, they are an extension of your feet and legs, and not hindering your performance.

The most honest advice that I can give on the subject of footwear is not to become attached to a pair of boots or shoes to the point that you wear them at every occasion simply because they are your "favorite pair of boots". Take an objective look at all that is available and make your decision based upon your intended purpose on the next hunt. Many hunters become attached to a name brand, and refuse to admit that they are miserable under all but ideal conditions.

In Alaska, the conditions will be ideal only if you are the game animal. Ball games have a tendency to get "rained out", but big game hunts get "rained on", along with the hunters of Alaska big-game.

Undergarments

Polyester, polypropylene, or other synthetic blends -- You are going to smell to high heaven after a couple of days, but garments made of polyester can easily be rinsed in a creek or lake and dried with minimal good weather. Cotton will be difficult to dry, and will suck the life out of you when wet, remember. There's lots of variety on the market, and you will only need one set of undergarments on most hunts.

Socks should be non-cotton, and should provide some padding to reduce shock and blistering of the feet. I'll say it again; you must baby your feet at every opportunity after they become wet. You will only make the mistake of neglecting your feet once; I can assure that.

Change into a "fresh" pair of socks daily once your feet have become wet. And always carry an extra pair that remains in your sleeping bag for the purpose of sleeping with totally dry feet. This is the main cause of uncomfortable sleep; going to bed in damp clothing. Never do it if you can help it.

Sleeping Bag

I have thrown this in because very few of us have sleeping bags that are capable of keeping us comfortable under extreme conditions. I will pass along what I know about sleeping bags:

- If it won't keep you warm if it is wet, leave it at home and buy one that will.

- It will need to weigh no more than four pounds or so if you will be backpacking it during your trip. A six pound bag is heavy, but can be justified if you will not be backpacking, or you will be exposed to extremely cold conditions.

- Most sleeping bags are rated at a "comfort range". This does not mean that you will be comfortable if the temperature reaches that range, however. It simply means that you will be alive and probably not get hypothermia at that temperature. To ensure that I will always be comfortable, I purchase a bag that is rated for twenty degrees colder than I will be expecting.

- I only purchase sleeping bags from a company called "Wiggy's". This company supplies sleeping bags to the special operations branches of the U.S. military. They are by far the best bags that are made today, and are affordable. With a *Wiggy*, if it claims to be a 0 degree bag, you will be "toasty" at 0 degrees! Even when the bag is damp! Contact them at www.wiggys.com

Headgear and Gloves

You will need a toboggan-style pullover to keep the chill off. I always sleep in mine regardless of the temperature. This practice will ensure that you will stay warmer and avoid the unnoticed chill that causes runny noses and sore throats. When hunting in August, roll it down to keep the light out of your eyes while trying to sleep, as it will still be light enough outside to see at 11:30 p.m.

To keep the elements from running down your face, it is advisable to wear a hat that will repel water. I wear one of those "outback" style hats made of pigskin, which is naturally water repellent. Whatever you are comfortable with is best, just as long as it is functional. I have yet to see a hunter show up in Alaska without a hat, and even if you abhor having something on top of your head, after having worn a certain hat on your Alaska adventure, I'm quite sure it will become a part of your personality once you return triumphantly to the "outside".

Wear gloves to keep your fingers warm, not dry. Waterproof gloves will cause your hands to sweat, so just try to keep your fingers warm. I am partial to wool mittens that can be folded back to expose my fingers. These will warm your hands even when wet as long as it is not below freezing. If you will surely be hunting in a cold environment, bring something insulated, and water repellent. Stay away from dark colors so that slight movements of your hands will not be blatantly noticeable to the animals that you will be hunting.

Raingear

Wow! There has really been a raingear explosion in the last ten years or so. One man couldn't possible test all of the products available, so we will keep it simple. Here's what I know:

- Rubber will keep all rain out, but trap all perspiration in.

- Claims of "waterproof, yet breathable" are only marginally accurate. Even "breathable" materials will trap moisture when activity level is high so don't expect a miracle.

- "Gore-Tex" is still relatively expensive, and I have experienced that it will only repel water for the first two years or so, after that, mine were unreliable.

- If you will be backpacking, your raingear will need to be ultra light.

- A poncho works well during short periods of heavy rain, and will cover you and your gear with minimal unpacking and garment changing. Ponchos allow air to flow underneath them because it is not form-fitted like a pair of pants or jacket.

I personally use an inexpensive and ultra-light rain jacket and pants made by "Frogg Toggs". These have yet to fail me after repeated abuse. Regardless of the brand you choose, you will be relying on them as a wind barrier as well as a moisture barrier, so they will need to be compact enough to fit into your daypack. Contact Frogg Toggs at www.froggtoggs.com.

If you leave your camp on a sunny day without rain gear, five times out of ten you will need it before the day is done. If you are fortunate enough to be dry at any time during your Alaska hunt, stay that way for as long as possible. Any dry moment in Alaska could be the last moment that you are dry in Alaska.

Shelter

On an outfitted hunt, the outfitter will likely be providing your "field accommodations", and they will most likely be adequate for the conditions that the outfitter will put you into. However, if you are a do-it-yourselfer, there are some things that you will need to know about the tent that you will bring to Alaska.

Here's what I know about tents:

- You get what you pay for.

- The protective barrier (rain fly) will need to cover the entire tent, not just the upper part of the tent as is common with many of the cheaper models. In addition, it is imperative that it be "factory seam taped" in order to keep the seams from becoming saturated with water and transferring that water to the sleeping hunter below.

- The lower waterproof portion should be waterproof up to at least six inches from the surface that is in direct contact with the ground.

- It helps if your tent is aerodynamic, as you may encounter high winds. These winds will rip apart a tent that has too high a profile. Read on...

- Lots of tie-downs to anchor the tent for maximum stability in high winds. You can giggle now, but you won't be giggling when you return from a day of hunting to find that your camp is spread out a half mile to the downwind direction. A glacial zephyr will sound like a tornado before it hits, and you will be hanging on for dear life from the inside of your tent if you are ever fortunate enough to experience one. Hence:

- Sturdy, yet flexible aluminum poles, and the more the better. If you are going into sheep or goat country, it had better be at least a three-pole tent.

I own a two-person low-profile tent with four poles. I have plenty of room for my gear on a solo hunt and it is equally comfortable for winter and fall hunting.

Pack and Frame

You will need to bring a backpack capable of hauling at least eighty pounds comfortably. I can think of very few hunts in Alaska that do not require an external frame that will haul meat and gear. An exception would be a brown bear hunt that would take place from a boat in the bays surrounding Kodiak Island, or maybe if you are only hunting for snowshoe hares. That's it.

Even in those situations it will be necessary to haul your personal belongings from one intermediate destination to the next, and that is done effortlessly with the help of a backpack. The external frame should be removable from the pack bag itself and the pack bag should have the capability to operate independently, using it's own secondary straps. This allows the frame to be used as a freighter for hauling meat bags. These bags will be lashed to the frame using a strong nylon cord.

I will go into more detail later about exactly how this is done, but for now let's ensure that you will bring a backpack to Alaska that is adequate for the duties it will be asked to perform. I will list some of the traits of a worthy pack and frame:

- Packs are rated in cubic inches of storage capacity. You will need a minimum of 4,000 cubic inches of such capacity.

- This sounds like a large number, but one cubic foot is 1,728 cubic inches.

- External pockets are a plus, as it becomes tiresome to remove half of the contents of your pack each time an item is required.

- As with tents, you will get what you pay for, so don't skimp on the details unless you will be skimping on the hunt as well. (Doubtful)

- The frame has a built-in shelf for stabilizing heavy loads. This will be necessary when stacking bags of meat on the frame. A shelf can be added to an existing frame if it does not already have one, but a shelf may be hard to find in the "Lower 48" for lack of demand. If you are here and need one, go to *Mountain View Sports*, in Anchorage.

- Keep the as-purchased weight of the pack (empty) to a minimum. This will be important on hunts that will require you to backpack for long distances. A five-pound pack is acceptable; a six or seven pound pack is extremely heavy.

- Always carry extra of the pins that support the weight of your bag. These bend and break at inopportune times, and if the wrong one fails, and you have no replacement, your hunt may be effectively over. If one pin on the same side fails twice, find the reason; usually there is a problem that can be easily remedied.

- I expect a Titanium frame to be out soon, if it is not already. This will be expensive, but it will be an acceptable expense because of the weight it will save.

I can't say enough about your pack's being one of the most important items that you will have with you on your hunt. But I don't know what more to say about them either. If you talk to someone who has hunted Alaska successfully, and he is happy with the pack that he used, then that is the one you want.

I use a Cabela's' Alaskan III, and to date it has been adequate under all circumstances that I have used it for. Seek www.cabelas.com.

Rifle

Touchy subject. Again, I will not alienate anyone by suggesting that a certain manufacturer is more advanced than another. We will simply discuss the traits of an adequate rifle or bow that will allow you to be successful. Here we go:

I like a blued rifle for inherent accuracy. I don't have any scientific findings to back this up; I just prefer steel to stainless steel for accuracy. The drawback to blue steel is heavier maintenance before, during, and after the hunt to ensure proper functioning and accuracy. I accept that drawback in order to hunt with a rifle that I am comfortable with.

Stainless steel, on the other hand, does not take away from the accuracy of a rifle, and requires less maintenance. Don't mistakenly misinterpret this as maintenance free, as all rifles require maintenance while in the field (bush). We will find hunters on both sides of this argument, so decide for yourself what you are more comfortable with.

I prefer a bolt-action to a pump or semiautomatic. A bolt-action rifle is more accurate at long ranges, but I will accept that a follow-up shot on a close grizzly bear would be a bit quicker with one of the alternatives. I have extensive training through the Marine Corps with a bolt-action rifle, and so will always seek a rifle of the type.

The recent advances in short-action (S.A.) calibers make a magnum or *ulti*-magnum caliber very attractive. I believe that S.A. is inherently more accurate than long-action (L.A.) and also is easier to manipulate when a speedy follow-up shot is warranted.

Trigger pull is very important to me. I have been conditioned to expect a crisp break. Most rifles when purchased, have adequate triggers to do the job, but I prefer a custom trigger job. If you are comfortable with your trigger, under all circumstances, then don't have it adjusted. And never, ever adjust a trigger just before a hunt, as you will surely squeeze off a round before intended when your "scope fills with hair".

The weight of your rifle, light or heavy, will only be a factor if you will be carrying it for long distances. Some ways to lighten a favorite, yet heavy rifle are to replace the stock with a lighter model, or replace the sling with a lighter one. Synthetic stocks are generally lighter and certainly less apt to warp in wet conditions. Leather slings are heavier than nylon slings and will absorb more water when wet. If your rifle is a "club", chances are you already know it, but don't come to that realization at 3,700 feet of altitude on the second day of packing to your sheep hunting location. The activity level of your hunt will be the determining factor in whether or not you need to replace your "club".

The caliber you choose to bring to Alaska will depend on what you intend to have a shot at while in Alaska. I will not attempt to bore you with what I do and do not know about ballistics.

Chances are you are already adept in the field to some extent. It will not be necessary to hand load your ammunition, as most of the ammunition that can be bought over the counter is sufficient to do the job as long as you understand the job that you are undertaking.

The idea in Alaska is to "anchor" the intended game animal at or very near where it is standing when your rifle fires. Professional guides do not like to track wounded game in Alaska and you will not either. Normally, a wounded game animal in Alaska will take you places that you would rather not go, and in some instances, like sheep or goats, where you cannot go. You can smile like a opossum when your grizzly crumbles with one well placed shot from your large, magnum caliber rifle, or you can fear for your life if he runs into an alder thicket because you were "under gunned" with a .30-06.

Here are my thoughts on rifles and calibers for Alaska game:

Note - All weights are live weight, on average, for mature representatives of the species.

Dall sheep (175 – 250 lbs)

Flat-shooting, hard-hitting calibers like .270, 7mm, or .300 Win. Mag. with light bullets do the trick. Accuracy is a must, and under no circumstances take a shot if you cannot recover your sheep where he stands or the area below him, as they have a tendency to take a tumble from accessible places, onto places that are inaccessible.

Mountain Goat (150 – 300 lbs)

Goats can take a tremendous amount of punishment, and if shot near a cliff or drop-off, they pull the dramatic "cowboy tumbling from the roof" stunt.   This happens almost without exception. You will want to shoot them in only an accessible spot and have him drop there if possible. I suggest 7mm or greater for this purpose. Most swear by a .338 for its brutal stopping power.

Caribou (250 – 450 lbs)

I would not hunt this species with less than a .270 caliber rifle. Within that or any caliber, I would not hunt with less than a 150-grain bullet. Bears live where caribou live, so you are even better off with a .30 caliber rifle. If your shot is properly placed, you will find that caribou will not run as far as a deer, as their flight instinct is not as acute.

Black Bear (250 – 550 lbs)

Black bears can take a great deal of shock, and will run hard if not hit properly. A .270 with a heavy bullet will do the job minimally, but don't show up for a guided black bear hunt with less than a .30 caliber rifle with heavy, hard hitting bullets. Chances are you will track your bear for at least thirty yards into thick brush.

Moose (900 - 1,600 lbs)

You are not going to believe what you've done when you walk up to your first bull moose on the ground. These critters are huge, and can take a well-placed shot and run with it. You will want him to "drop anchor" on a dry spot of ground, so do not insult him with less than a .30 caliber rifle with a heavy bullet. You will want a deep penetrating bullet, and your goal is not to recover the bullet, but to make two holes; one entry and a little bit larger exit. This sounds brutal, but bones broken in the process are a plus.

Grizzly or Brown Bear (450 – 1,400 lbs)

You've undoubtedly heard the expression, "come loaded for bear". Well, I can bet that Alaska is where that originated. If your rifle is not a magnum caliber, and you don't intend to buy another rifle, then you will need to cancel the hunt. Personally, I prefer, as many hunters do, a .375 H&H or a .338 at least. You will be seeking bone crushing penetration and maximum vital tissue damage. A bear of this species can finish you with one swipe of a massive paw. If you give him that opportunity because you did not place your shot well, he will travel on adrenalin alone to get to the threat. The threat being YOU. Finish the bear with follow up shots until there is no movement.

Bison (1,000 – 2,000 lbs)

If you are fortunate enough to draw one of these lottery tags, consider it a tag of a lifetime. If you are additionally fortunate enough to get one in your sights, let's hope that you've got a lot of stopping power. Heavy magnum is a must, unless you are a traditionalist, then you're going to need a lot of black powder, or maximum draw weight from your bow.

The bison in Alaska cohabitate with the moose so be sure of what you have in your sights before the rifle jerks in your hands; by then it will be too late.

Archery Equipment

If you are considering bringing a bow to Alaska, it can go without saying that you must have acquired enough knowledge and experience necessary to take such a bold measure. As for the archery equipment that you bring to Alaska, there simply are no horrible bows on the market any more due to the keen competition in such a rapidly expanding market. The only important factor I would bring to light is draw weight. You will need to work your way up to the most that you can hold with your bow and shoot comfortably and accurately. Penetrating a moose will be like shooting through a refrigerator filled with meat, so don't show up with the same equipment that you take to your white-tailed deer stand. Your shafts and broad heads will need to be the top of the line, and your nerves sharpened as to be sharper than your blades because you will not believe the size of the animals that you will need to be within thirty yards of (shooting range). Think of the shivers you will get in the presence of a large bull moose if you get shivers with a buck under your stand. I hear it's called "buck fever", well in Alaska; your fever will develop quickly into full-blown "pneumonia"!

Optics

Binoculars will be absolutely necessary. A scope for your rifle may not be, depending on how evolved you are within the species, *humanus ballisticanus*. I know of many excellent riflemen that still prefer open sights, and the game animals are bigger here, so why add complication to simplicity if you are accustomed to open sights.

Riflescope -- As for the quality of your riflescope, bring what you shoot well and you'll do fine. I shoot a variable, and 10x is its highest range. For anything that you cannot identify with the highest setting on your variable, you will need to be looking through a spotting scope, anyway. Clear, bright scopes are the rule, with a reticle that will stick out in low light conditions. Most dedicated riflemen are also dedicated to one particular brand or another, just ask someone with some experience; but Not a salesman! Salesmen are often pushed to move scopes that are laggards, or to make room for newer models.

Your favorite rifle scope will be getting wet, and most likely, it will get banged around a bit, so ensure that you have quality bases as well as a removable scope cover.

Binoculars -- Bring clear, bright binoculars that will maintain their focal abilities under extreme circumstances; extremely cold and extremely wet, for instance. Your budget is your limit, but purchase the best that you can afford because you definitely get what you pay for where lenses are concerned. If your activity will be sheep or goat hunting, then you will need to consider lighter versions of the original. Be careful with compact binoculars, though, as looking at the deer mount at the other end of the sporting goods section will differ greatly from spending hours upon endless hours glassing for shadows amidst the rocks and cliffs. Compact binoculars make me cross-eyed if I look through them long enough.

I find a thirty-millimeter objective lens sufficient for most of the glassing that I do. If a binocular is called an "8x30", then the "30" is the diameter of the objective lens. The "8" is the magnification. I find that most "7x50's" are rather heavy for my taste, so I stick with the former. By the way, Dall sheep will be looking back at you through "8x20's". They've got you pegged most of the time before you leave the airport at Anchorage! – Haah!

Spotting Scope -- A spotting scope can save you a day's worth of walking in most situations. If you have a particular trophy quality in mind, then you will need an "optic brick" to put into your pack; that's what I call a spotting scope on a hunt in which I didn't get to use it! A magnification of 45x should be a maximum, and will get you close when you are actually miles away. A tripod is optional only if you are adept at balancing a spotting scope on your pack, but you just can't beat a tripod for comfortable, stable viewing if you will not be walking for a couple of days to your hunting site. In the latter case, I personally can't justify the extra weight. The tripod sits perfectly next to that stump in your moose camp, though, and I never go on a fly-in hunt without one.

GPS (Global Positioning System)

They are relatively cheap compared to five years ago, and much easier to learn to use, so buy one and learn how to use it. If you get fogged out of your camp as can happen on a moment's notice, you will be forever thankful that you have one in order to find your way back. In this case, a GPS will do the thinking, and all you will need to do is follow the direction arrow; however, a GPS, even when used effectively, is not a replacement for a thorough understanding of land navigation and the ability to read a map.

There will be a gear list discussed in a later chapter, so we won't go into the fine details now. I simply wanted to give you an idea of the kind of large expense items that it may be necessary to purchase soon after you've purchased your ticket to Alaska.

Remember, confidence in the gear that you bring will be more important than the price tag on the gear that you bring. Become comfortable with your entire gear inventory and adept at using it prior to your arrival in your hunting area.

Once this plane departed, a little gear and a lot of confidence was all that Dewayne Craig was left with.

This smile is worth a thousand words. I think an "outsider" fell in love with Alaska at about this moment.

Preparation

Gearing up for the trip will not be difficult; gearing *yourself* up for the trip however, will be a different story. Eliminate the anxious anticipation and nervous excitement you are experiencing about coming to Alaska, and what you have left is what needs to be developed, or programmed. Anticipation and excitement don't win marathons; mental and physical preparation wins marathons.

Mental

I'm not going to launch into a feeble attempt to convince you that a hunt in Alaska will be akin to running a marathon, but I will tell you that in order to be successful in Alaska, a certain amount of "psyching yourself up" will be necessary. I once had a close hunting buddy stand on a floatplane dock and tell me about all of the distractions that he had experienced in the recent months before his trip to Alaska. I asked if he was pumped about coming up to get his first bull moose, and his reply was something to the effect that he "wouldn't be too surprised if he didn't connect because he had been on many a hunt like this that ultimately didn't turn out successful".

A dear friend was standing here full of negative energy on his way to a trophy moose hunt, and it just about tore me apart. I stepped a couple of steps away just in case something tried to rub off on me, though. It did not surprise me, only nine short days later when he was the only one in our hunting party of three who did not take a moose.

Now I don't profess to be a *Zen master*, or even *a Zen follower* for that matter, but I do know that filling yourself with negative energy before an endeavor will almost always bring about a negative result. It's kind of like *manifest destiny*; which is where you fill someone else so full of energy, positive or negative, that they will begin to transform that energy into action.

I know this from parenting; if you tell your marginally talented kid that he is the most talented kid in the world and you are so proud of him, he will become even more asserted in his endeavors, and thus more talented. You provided the path to destiny, and the kid manifested, or realized that destiny. If you are the kind of parent who tells your kid how much of a "screw up" she is, then I can almost guarantee you without knowing either one of you that you have a screwed up kid that will go out of her way to show you just how "screwed up" she can get. Mental energy converted to words, then converted to actions. What's left now is for you to convince yourself that it will be possible for you to travel to Alaska and bring back exactly what you are after.

Positive mental preparedness will be the most important aspect of your pre-trip planning. This will involve surrounding yourself with thoughts of what exactly a successful hunt will be for you. It will be unrealistic to imagine coming to Alaska to take the next world record barren ground caribou, so just imagine taking a representative bull with palmated antlers, for instance. This, you can make into a reality. The next world record will eventually fall into someone's scope, but that happens more as a matter of chance than as a matter of research and skill.

Envisioning and living the hunt even before you step onto the airplane will start with active research to learn everything that you can about the species that you will be pursuing. You should be determined to rent every videotape you can find on the subject, and spend time in libraries and bookstores searching for glimpses of the trophy that you will be seeking. I make a concerted effort to "connect" with the very animal that will come into my sights even before having physically seen him, and I start this "connection" as soon as I begin to feel the anticipation build. In drawing his likeness to you in your thoughts and dreams, you will be surprised at how close you can draw him to you in the reality. Call me crazy if you like, but my friends call me successful. I attribute this success to my mental preparedness, not my prowess.

Physical

Now let's talk about that marathon --

Simply put, you will not be "hunting hard" in Alaska if you come up for your dream hunt without a certain amount of physical preparedness; you will come to Alaska and have a "hard hunt"! Getting yourself in acceptable physical shape will allow you to access game with less effort, thereby putting you in a better position to be successful.

I will not attempt at this point to dictate a training regimen to you that will prepare you for anything and will carry you to each corner of Alaska. I will, however, describe situations that you will find yourself in at some time during your trip. The exception to this rule is in the case that you are hiring a guide to do your hunting for you; where all you will do is pull the trigger on your rifle, or string on your bow. I'm sure that the guide will have a cadre of lesser guides who will skin, quarter, and haul your meat out for you as well; in this case all that will be required for you to exercise will be the smiling muscles in your face so you don't pull one when photographed beaming, crouched behind your downed "conquest".   Remember, you purchased the book entitled, *"Hunting Hard –"*, not, *"Hardly Hunting...In Alaska?"*

Walking – At minimum, on my fly-out hunts I still manage to walk to and from my vantage point, which is where I attempt to view game. This will require that I walk a minimum of three miles in a day. Let me warn you, walking in Alaska is not like mall walking. You will be crawling under, over, and through brush, so even in this minimal activity you will need strong ankles, knees and calf muscles that have been conditioned to walking on uneven ground. If you are on the *low-ground* of Alaska, you will experience muskeg, which is boggy, spongy ground that sinks beneath your feet. This will require you to lift your knees with each step in order to plant your foot on the next patch of boggy, spongy ground that sinks. This *low-ground* walking will likely take place in hip waders, which require considerably more effort to walk in than do hiking or hunting boots. Become comfortable in the hip waders, because we call them "Alaskan Sneakers".

On the *high ground* of Alaska, you will be doing what we call "side-hilling", which means walking around a mountain somewhere on its slopes. This activity will be torture on your ankles, especially with a load, if you have not conditioned and strengthened them. It is much more tiring than walking on uneven ground and can only be avoided by walking straight up or down hill.

Uphill will require leg strength, flexibility, and endurance. Additionally, conditioning of your lungs to sustain this activity will be essential to avoid long stops at short intervals. If you have read the stories in the first part of this book, you'll remember my tearing a calf muscle while packing a sheep uphill. I cannot stress enough that this will be murderous on your body if you are not in the shape to carry out this activity.

Downhill is much more painful to me than uphill, it's sort of like what they call "negative rep's" in the gym. On my last sheep hunt we did these reps for two days at ten hours a day in order to get back to level ground, which leaves a lasting impression on the tendons of your knees for about six weeks.

In order of importance, I would say that the following would be necessary in order to do the walking activities of an Alaska hunt and keep from injuring yourself:

1) Flexibility conditioning of muscles, joints and tendons
2) Endurance conditioning with a moderately weighted pack
3) Strength training

Backpacking – Expect a week's worth of provisions and gear to weigh sixty to seventy pounds. This activity will get you to places that simply cannot be reached by airplane; which will expose you to game that only the hardiest of hunters will reach. This means of hunting can also be limiting in that you must not only pack in but you must also pack out, and under the best of conditions, having been successful, your pack on the way out will weigh twice or more what it did on the way in.

Rule number one; it is not prudent to begin a backpacking hunt for bull moose, period. Stay close to your camp and let them come to you. If you walk for three miles to down a moose, you will spend the better part of a week with a pack on your back that will weigh at least eighty or so pounds. At nine round trips for a moose, you are looking at *fifty-four* miles of backpacking (9packs x3miles x2trips) to get the entire animal back to your starting point. A caribou can be packed out in two to four pack loads, depending on how you like to pace yourself, so you make that call. There are very few places where a non-resident can hunt caribou from a road system, anyway, so just keep an eye on your GPS to determine how far you are from your camp on your fly-in.

By now you get the picture associated with backpacking on a hunt in Alaska. Just read the "Walking" section above, and add a pack. I won't even mention Dall sheep or mountain goats, because a non-resident under most circumstances must hire a guide to hunt these game animals; and I guarantee you won't find a guide who will be packing you in to a hunt, because there is no price that can be put on that much misery, and if there is, you can't afford it. The exception to this rule would be a goat or sheep hunt that is near the road system, and even that is left to the "hardiest of the hardy". If you are a non-resident coming to

Alaska for a *strictly backpacking* Dall sheep or mountain goat hunt, I have a question for you: When was your last marathon, and did you hit the magical 3-hour mark?

Hint: Let's find us a good flight service, and our knees just might live as long as we do.

Training is crucial during the off-season. Sessions such as this one easily transform traditional training into a rewarding experience.

Doing Your Homework

Unlike the homework that you learned to dread in school, doing your homework for a planned hunt in Alaska will be a pleasure, and will help to occupy that void of time between your commitment to the hunt and departure for the hunt. The homework involved is simply learning as much as you possibly can about the area that you will be hunting, as well as the area you won't be hunting in; that would be the "remainder" of Alaska. This activity is entirely self-paced, and can become extremely addicting, so be careful.

Start by ordering a copy of the hunting regulations from the Alaska Department of Fish and Game. The new regulations come available in June of each year and are current through May of the following year. This booklet is first of all, "the law", and secondly, is full of helpful information on the species and location that you will be hunting. Contact: Alaska Department of Fish and Game

P.O. Box 25526

Juneau, AK 99802-5526

(907) 465-4100 www.state.ak.us/adfg

If you have already chosen a flight service to get you to the game animals, ask which Game Management Unit they will likely be flying you to for your hunt. There are twenty-six units, which are further broken down into subunits. It will be necessary at some point to know the specific subunit that you will be hunting as this will dictate the "rules of engagement". The laws differ vastly from unit to unit and sub-unit to subunit, much as the laws differ from state to state, and it is your responsibility to follow the laws.

Of course, the flight service that you have chosen will help you to uphold the game laws but they will not be held ultimately responsible, you will. Research first, and then ask questions. Please don't call the flight service and ask them to read the regulations to you as *they will dread your arrival*! Questions that arise from your reading of the regulations must only be directed to the Alaska Department of Fish and Game as clarity and interpretation is best learned at the source. I once bought a permit to hunt a wolf as an incidental while on my caribou hunt; only to find that I didn't need a wolf permit in my particular subunit. I spent money that I didn't have to spend because I failed to properly interpret the regulations as they pertained to my sub-unit.

Your hunting license may be purchased through the mail, or online in advance of your hunt. In the case that you are a procrastinator, you may purchase your license within Alaska at any place of business that carries sporting goods. If you still have questions upon arrival, it is a terrific idea to visit the nearest office of the Alaska Department of Fish and Game to get your questions answered. They offer trophy recognition videos and videos about the proper care of your meat and trophy which will become invaluable whether the bull moose is in your sights or on the ground in front of you. Remember to make sure someone gets a picture of the look on your face when you see your first bull moose on the ground; it's priceless!

Once you've memorized the hunting regulations for the entire State of Alaska, and you can recite it better than you can the Gettysburg Address, (Just kidding, of course!) you're ready for the next step; ordering maps.

I am a topography nut. I get "sucked in" by the contour lines of a map and can literally look at maps for hours. It helps that I have a healthy background in land navigation through the Marine Corps, but even if you don't, you've got to admit, they look pretty fascinating, right? Land navigation is a necessary fundamental of hunting in Alaska, so if you're serious about hunting in Alaska, you'll take the time to learn something about how to read a map.

I would grow old before I could pass along all I know about land navigation in this book, so you'll need to do some investigating for yourself. There are excellent books on the subject in libraries and bookstores alike, and if you cannot find any, just ask that Marine or Army buddy of yours to give you some tips.

Try to get a detailed map of your hunting area if you can manage to; it will provide hours of blank staring, as if you are waiting for a bull caribou to jump right off the page or something. Once you've learned to tell a *draw* from a *finger*, you'll learn to associate terrain features with their representative symbols on the map, and maybe save yourself a great deal of unnecessary backtracking or climbing if you are on one of those kind of hunts.

I honestly and truthfully never, ever go into an area unless I've first committed a mental picture of the map to memory. This is extremely effective in making you feel comfortable in what will be vast, immense country.

Dan Presley, of Alaska, certainly did his homework before packing, with three horses, more than 75 miles in search of this 75-inch bull of a lifetime.

My "homework" is never ending, as I plan to hunt in every corner of this great state of Alaska. Your desire to research should stem from curiosity and a yearning to know more about the area that you will be creating lifelong memories in. With time and experience, the research that you do out of curiosity will begin to be productive, eventually opening doors to other areas and opportunities to hunt.

I owe my second Dall sheep to a map session with a couple of buddies; we were arguing the accessibility to a certain portion of a mountain range because of a seemingly formidable river that necessitated crossing.

The map session caused us to take a road trip to view the area firsthand. We liked the looks of the area, so we chartered a bush plane to fly us over the range. During the flight we spotted a band of six Dall rams in one of the accessible drainages, three of which appeared to be legal. That is how hunts are made here in Alaska. Weeks later we set out, with the opening of season only two days away. The river crossing proved to be a non-event, but the hike to the sheep is painfully memorable. Five days later we returned triumphantly with two full-curl Dall sheep rams!

Who says homework doesn't pay off later in life?!

I almost pulled a cheek muscle after taking my second Dall ram.

A triumphant hunter rides the floats over to the meat cache as our Mulchatna caribou hunt winds down. Will this be you... next year?

Finalizing the Plans

This will be a critical juncture in the success of your trip and will probably happen at the thirty-day mark before you depart. It is necessary to get last-minute things in order to avoid a "frantic" departure. The idea is to relax during the period just before your departure, not anxiously pace back and forth worrying about what you may be forgetting. Here are some things to look forward to when departure is nearing:

If you will be using a guide or air taxi service, your final payment will be due on or near this date. Once you are standing outside the bush plane, loading your rifle and pack, you will be hoping that your pilot is going to be good to you by delivering on everything that you have been "promised". In order for this to happen, you will have to make good on your commitments first. Become a preferred customer and you will receive preferred treatment. I have lots of friends in the business of putting hunters on or near game, and I know that they have high respect for the hunting parties with their "stuff together".

If you are staying overnight anywhere along your route, then have a confirmation number in hand. Contact a representative of the outfit that you will be staying with to ensure things are in order. Do not show up on check-in day to be told that there are no rooms available, because there will also be no rooms available anywhere else either. Secure a late check-in at this time if need be.

Hopefully you are holding your airline tickets in hand. Since the advent of "ticket-less" tickets makes this less probable, call to confirm your itinerary and that your flights are still scheduled at the times and on the dates they were purchased for. I know it sounds "funny", but there are a lot of *bizarre* changes happening daily in the airline industry. Call to give yourself *peace of mind* to avoid standing at the counter giving them a *piece of your mind*, which will do no good once the damage has been done to your plans. Remember to inquire about changes in the amount of allowable baggage that you will be traveling with.

How will you get your antlers and meat home if you connect with the trophy of your dreams? This needs to be hammered out now, not in a mad scramble three hours before your flight back. Get recommendations from the air taxi, guide, and the air cargo service that you will be using.

Arrange for your backpack to be mailed to your home by ensuring that you will have access to a post office in Alaska. Special note: The U.S. Post Office at the Ted Stevens International Airport in Anchorage is always open; 24hours, 7 days, 365 days a year. Open 366 during leap year!

Is your rifle lubricated to protect it against the weather? Are you happy with the way it shot the last time you had it at the range? Now is the time to answer these questions.

Finally, this is the time to meet with your hunting buddies, with all of your major gear along, to ensure that everyone has the basic necessities to carry out the hunt. *This* is the opportune time to find out what is missing. Also decide what gear will be shared to keep the travel weight at a minimum. Tents, stoves and spotting scopes should be shared; *sleeping bags should not....*Hmmmmnnn

Bob Sadowski and I get in one last conditioning hike during moose season.

Last-minute Checklist

The following details should be tended to approximately thirty days prior to your departure to Alaska:

- Reconfirm all legs of airline travel.
- Settle all payments with services at your destination.
- Make phone calls to confirm reservations in Alaska. (Hotel, rental van, etc.)
- Go over gear lists with other members of your hunting party to eliminate redundant gear and excess weight.
- Sight-in your rifle or bow before packing it for the trip.
- Arrange for fuel for your camp stove. Remember, it cannot fly commercially.
- Store ammunition in proper container for air travel.
- Hunting licenses are purchased or arranged for; if purchased already, they should be stored securely within your packed gear.
- Remind your taxidermist and meat processor of your anticipated return date.

Lastly, but most important, **think positively**! You are coming to Alaska to be successful in your hunt, so begin to surround yourself with positive, successful thoughts. Envision your hunt as you want it to happen, even down to making a mental connection with the very animal that you will be coming to hunt!

Packing for Your Trip

You're almost there; just this one monumentally important task left before you can begin to enjoy your journey to "The Last Frontier". That statement makes the task sound like drudgery, but actually packing for your trip can be very enjoyable.

Start by making yourself a packing list. This is made easy if you group items into categories based upon your activity. I will attempt to guide you through this process, but your comforts and likes will surely be different from mine, therefore we will not attempt to make an all inclusive packing list. The disclaimer, "may include but is not limited to", will apply to the gear that may fall within the following categories:

For the hunt -- These are the items that will be the tools of the hunt. I list them first because they are the most important to the success of the hunt itself as they are required for the taking of game.

Included are:

Rifle	License	Bow
Ammunition	Game Harvest Tags	Quiver/Arrows
Cleaning Gear*	Identification	Release or Tab
Camera*		

***Seek out a *"Bore Snake"*, by *Michael's of Oregon*, in the caliber that you will be hunting with. This is a long, braided cleaning wick that is pulled through your bore. The *Bore Snake* is excellent for removing debris and moisture from your barrel. Both will deposit there at some time during your hunt, trust me.

Pre-lubricate small rags for wiping the exterior surface of your rifle after torrential downpours and the like. It is imperative to take good care of your most important tool so it will function as it was designed when the shot of a lifetime presents itself.

***Document your hunt with pictures; many of them. When I took my first Dall Sheep I forgot my camera in my base camp! I am still kicking myself for that mistake. Ensure that your camera is light, and has a built-in flash for low-light conditions. If your camera is too heavy, you will always find a way to leave it behind. There are self-winding, auto-focus cameras out that are light and relatively affordable.

Camping and Shelter – These are the items that will stay at your base camp. They are necessary if you will **not** be hunting from a lodge or cabin, which is sometimes the case on guided hunts. If you will not be staying in a structure, you will need the following as a minimum:

Tent, complete	Stove*	Utensils
Sleeping Pad	Cooking Vessel	Bug Juice/Headnet

*** Fuel for your stove must be purchased or otherwise arranged for at an intermediate destination prior to your reaching the hunting area. You will not be allowed to take any kind of fuel on domestic or international airline flights under any circumstance, and your journey will end abruptly if you try to smuggle it on in your luggage. Plan time at your destination to purchase fuel for your stove, and ensure that the fuel is compatible with the model stove that you are relying on. Your stove may require brand-specific fuel because it threads or clamps onto your stove, so make sure that you get it right the first time. I have mentioned before that fuel may be transported by the flight service that you may be using to get to the bush, but you must declare it! Do not endanger the lives of everyone involved by stowing away your fuel canisters!

***Stoves with igniters attached are a big plus, provided that the igniter works. Check this before you rely on it.

Clothing Needs – We will discuss only the clothes that will be packed for your travel, as you will surely be wearing a traveling set for all non-hunting activities. This set that you wear should include a lightweight water-proof or resistant jacket. This will keep you from digging into your bags upon arrival in inclement weather. Don't worry; we all wear jackets nearly all the time up here, so you won't look out of place -- Here are the basics:

Underwear (2)	Hunting Hat	Outer Pants (2)
Socks (4)	Wool Toboggan	Long Underwear
Hunting Footwear	Rain/Wind Suit	Fleece Sleeping Clothes
Glove Liners	Gloves	Fleece Layering Clothes

***I can't stress enough the fact that you should try to leave as much *cotton* at home as possible. That includes flannel, sweatshirts, workout suits, underwear, T-shirts and socks. Some of you will call me to tell me how impressed you were that you were never cold and almost always felt dry because you wore polyester blends or wool; those of you that learn the hard way will not call, but you will leave the cotton at home next time, I can guarantee that.

Hunting Accessories – These are the items that will aid in your hunt and will increase your chances for success. Pick and choose according to your needs utilizing some of the information that you have read or will soon read in the remaining chapters of this book. Important items include:

Spotting Scope w/ Tripod	Moose Call*	Rangefinder
Binoculars	Scope Cover	
Global Positioning System	Map of Hunting Area	

***Absolutely recommended that you learn to use one if you will be hunting Moose. That is, if your guide will not be doing the calling for you. More later on this...

Field-Dressing Gear – Once the animal is down, these will be necessary to get it back to a location near your camp.

Folding Knife*	Game Bags	Ground White Pepper, 1 lb
Sheath Knife*	Extra Lashing	Kosher Salt
Honing Steel*	Folding Saw	

***Knives with long, tapered points tend to puncture capes quicker than do skinning style knives. I prefer a "drop point" knife for skinning and caping, and a longer, sheath knife for removing meat from the bone.   A butcher's "boning knife" works the absolute best for removing meat from the bone. See if you can take one along, even if you have to make a simple sheath for it out of cardboard and duct tape.

***A small, portable honing steel is necessary to keep and edge on your blade. It is not necessary to carry stones and oil; the honing steel will do the same job or better, occupying minimal space and weighing very little. Again, www.cabelas.com for this little gem.

Miscellaneous Equipment – This is a very broad category, and can include nearly every piece of gear imaginable, so my advice is not to get carried away and make sure most everything has a dual purpose.

Headlamp*   Simple First Aid Kit*   Lip Balm

Batteries*   Signal Mirror   Lighter/Matches

Pen Flares*   Water Purifier*   Duct Tape*

Water Bottles (2) *Hip Waders   Small Candle*

***Headlamps offer hands-free operation, which is a must for doing the dirty work of eviscerating game as well as moving through thick brush after dark.

***All batteries should be interchangeable; that is, if your GPS operates on AA batteries, then your flashlight or headlamp should also operate on AA batteries.

***Survival stories are plentiful in Alaska. In order to be rescued in the event of a debilitating fall or tragedy you must be able to signal your rescuers. I always carry pen flares and a signal mirror "just in case". It is possible to die or succumb to hypothermia while a helicopter does circles a few miles away if you have no way to notify the helicopter of your location.   Be prepared!

***Bring only a "tried and true" water purifier to Alaska.   Do not show up with a water purifier that you have not, or don't effectively know how to use.   Make sure that the rate of flow will support the required amounts that you will be attempting to draw through the filter.   It is no fun to sit at the water's edge for more than an hour each day gathering water for the hunting party.   If you are on a party hunt, make sure that there is more than one purifier on the trip.   One will surely fail, as this is not the most reliable piece of gear that you will have on the trip.

***Don't waste your money on expensive water bottles that have insulated covers and fastening loops attached.   "Bottled water" bottles purchased from a convenience store work wonderfully; just make sure that you have a smaller one that is always close, and a larger one of maybe two liters or so to get you through most of a day.   This will keep you from filling up so often, and also ensure that you have more than a small amount of water available for the times you will be separated from any water source.

***Wrap one of your water bottles with 10 feet or so of duct tape. It will come in handy for an assortment of uses.   I immediately put a small piece over the crown of my barrel to keep water and debris out.   This can be removed prior to the shot, or the shot can be taken with the tape on if absolutely necessary, but on a very short range shot only.

Duct tape can be used to stop the formation of a blister on your foot if you apply the tape before the hot spot actually turns into a blister.   If you experience a burning sensation on a foot while walking, find and fix the problem. Often it is as simple at retying your boot or shoe laces.

***In your first aid kit, you must include a disinfectant cream to stop bacterial infection. Also include small bandages and band-aids for small cuts that will happen as a result of dense brush and excessive handling of knives. You will not be prepared for a major medical emergency, so ensure that you do not cause one!

***If you light a small candle in your tent a while before you go inside, it will be much warmer inside, provided there is not a lot of wind through your tent. Be careful not to burn your shelter down!

Toiletries and Sanitary Items – Self explanatory, right?
Includes:

Cotton Wash Towel	Small Soap	Sandwich Bags*
Toilet Tissue*	Shaving Gear*	Disinfectant Wipes
Tooth Brush/Paste	Garbage Bags*	

*** *Condition* yourself to using paper towels instead of toilet tissue, if you are one of those people who can stand to. Paper towels will take up much less space, as you will only need to take two or three for each day in the bush. They are much more versatile and don't disintegrate when they come in contact with moisture. *Conditioning* is the key word here, so experiment before leaving the comfort of your home.

***Leave your shaving gear at the place that you will come to when you depart the bush. The only photo opportunities available will require a "gruff", unshaven appearance. Hey, this is Alaska!

***Garbage bags will waterproof much of your gear and serve their intended purpose of collecting garbage.

***Not the sandwiches, just the bags. You will keep tags, ammunition, and all small items in them to keep the items dry.

Food – It is a great idea to shop for these items once you are in Alaska. But the important thing to remember is to pack them prior to going into the bush. Do not show up at the plane with grocery sacks for the pilot to load!

Here are my thoughts on food items to consider and the reason to consider them:

Freeze-dried meals – Light, complete, just need boiling water. They are not usually calorie packed, but you can supplement them with other items that will be mentioned. I purchase and carry one for each day afield, plus two extras.

Instant Noodles – These are the of the *Ramen Noodle* variety. They should not be considered to be energy-packed, but they are very comforting when it is cold. The warm broth will aid in hydrating you and warming you. A package usually holds me over until I can prepare a larger meal, and are supplemented with a *Power Bar*, as a light lunch.

Fats – Dried Cheeses like parmesan cheese or even a small block of cheddar make great flavor additions to your meal, and they are packed with calories, protein and calcium.

Dried Fruit – You will want the tartness of dried fruit to break up the monotony as well as to provide vitamin C and bulk to your diet. Most grocery stores carry them in bulk. I usually take a mix of bananas, cranberries, raisins and apple.

Nuts – All nuts are not nutritionally equal. I am partial to cashews for taste, fat content, and they are additionally rich in vitamin B. These are great to nibble on just before you drift off to sleep as they provide fat-rich calories to keep you warm for most of the night.

Nutritional Bars – "*Power Bars*" are my favorite, and they now come in excellent flavors. I use these as a "pick-me-up" between meals. They have a certain way of bringing me out of a slump when my energy level is low and they don't require the effort of preparing a full meal.

Breakfast Cereal Mix – I have a ratio of the following ingredients that I particularly like. This is an excellent breakfast boost that I mix and store in gallon freezer bags. Boil water and then add the mix to your water and you have a breakfast that will carry you well into mid-morning. Here are the ingredients:
Quick Oatmeal   "Fruit and Fiber" brand cereal with nuts
Wheat Germ   Brown Sugar   Powdered Milk
Dry Creamer
Raisins *or* Fresh Blueberries if I can find them near my camp

Drink mixes – I carry powdered *Gatorade*, dry coffee, and a couple of cocoa packets. Tea bags, especially flavored ones with lemon or mint really come in handy when the flavor of coffee would be too strong. All of these can be heated, including the Gatorade, which is excellent served warm at breakfast, or at bedtime. The point to this is that you will definitely want something more than water, as water alone will be dreadfully boring after a few days. I have carried a lemon to the bush before, and cut off a piece into my water supply to add some flavor. It really hit the spot at the time.

Vitamin Supplements – Don't leave home without them, and on especially grueling hunts, I take mega-doses of vitamin E to help repair muscles that are overworked. I also carry Ibuprofen to soften the pain of overworked muscles, but be careful only to take supplements with food, as they require food for proper absorption into the bloodstream.

That's it; I carry nothing else in the way of food unless I will be in a super- plush campsite. Maintaining proper nutrition during times of physical exertion will be one of the more important functions that you perform. If you take care of your muscles, they will gladly pack your meat and antlers for you; if not, they will fail you at the most inopportune times.

Clean Change of Clothes – For the "after the bush" endeavors; or "The Bush" after; whichever you prefer. This will include a dry pair of shoes or boots that did not go on the hunt. If you don't bring these, you may likely travel home with uncomfortable, wet feet. Once you have cleaned up, you will feel like a new person, because you're clean again, and because you have conquered an opportunity to hunt "The Great State of Alaska"!

We just discussed what to bring. It is equally important to discuss the manner in which you pack, as it will make for a smoother transaction at the ticket counter, provided you take some of the following advice regarding your allowable baggage:

Rifle Case – This must be a rugged, lockable case. I prefer heavy-gauge aluminum for its durability and the protection that it affords my rifle and scope. Into this case you will put your rifle, sling, knives, and optics. Remove the bolt from the rifle to put the security personnel at ease. That's it, lock it up.

It will be necessary to insert an "Unloaded Weapon" declaration into your rifle case at the ticket counter, so be prepared to do so. You will be declaring that your weapon is unloaded, and that your ammunition is packed in its original container, or a container that is specifically designed to hold ammunition. Loose ammunition rolling around your pack or case will not be permitted, and will get you in trouble at the X-ray machine, so don't do it!

Backpack – All of your ammunition and hunting and camping gear will go into or securely fastened onto your pack. Any gear that is attached to the outside must be securely fastened to the pack or you will be repacking at the terminal, so get it right. At the ticket counter, ask for a heavy plastic bag to enclose your pack in, this will keep the baggage handling personnel from handling it by the straps, causing you to loose gear. Again – No fuel for the stove on airline flights!

Second Checked Bag – This will contain your change of clothes, your hip waders, and any things that didn't fit into your backpack. Your sleeping bag would be a good candidate for this. Do not embarrass yourself by showing up with a huge duffel bag with seventy pounds of extras in it.

Carry-on Bag – This will contain water, your camera, shaving kit, a light jacket, and this book. It is important that you have your camera with you in your carry-on bag to document the trip and because the X-ray machine that all checked luggage must now go through will ruin your film. The X-ray machine at the gate, where your carry-on will be scanned by is much less powerful, and thus less damaging to your film.

There are "rights" and "wrongs" of packing ammunition. Do not pack it in the same container as your rifle, as you will surely be asked to repack your gear at the ticket counter. Instead, pack any and all ammunition in your backpack, which will be checked into the plane as baggage. Again, all ammunition must be in its original container or a container specifically designed to hold ammunition.   Your case will need to be opened at the ticket counter in order that an "Unloaded Weapon Declaration" card is placed beside your rifle. The card can be read through an X-ray machine, and will assure the airline professionals that you too are a professional, so make sure it's true.

Much more than this and you will know you've got too much gear! Each of your bags will be allowed to weigh no more than seventy pounds, and it should not come close to that weight. Remember to remove all pocket knives, and non-permissible items from your person prior to reaching the ticket counter to ensure a smooth check-in process.

As a single traveling hunter, you are representing all traveling hunters in the way that you conduct yourself during your trip. Enjoy your trip, but do not force the fact that you are exercising your hunting privileges on everyone that you come in contact with. Only fellow hunters will share your excitement, so remember to respect the opinions of the non-hunters, even though their views may not be your own.

These ewes allowed me to approach to within twenty-yards on a winter conditioning hike in my "back yard".

Speaking of packing; Dan Presley used pack-horses to get his trophy bull moose out of the bush. Once the "Last Frontier" gets a hold of you, you'll do whatever it takes to make your dreams come true.

Upon Arrival...

This is it – You're finally here. If you have flown into Anchorage, first take the time to see the wildlife displays at the airport. You have probably waited a very long time for this moment, so make sure that you have the presence of mind to enjoy it at a leisurely pace. Hopefully you have planned extra days at the beginning and at the end of this hunt. Use those days to ensure that things are on track as you have planned and envisioned them, and to enjoy the sights and people at your point of entry into the great state of Alaska.

You should be afforded a shuttle to pick up you and your belongings from the airport. There will be no rental vehicles left at the airport unless you have secured one in advance. If you have a couple of days to burn up, call around to the lesser popular rental establishments, and be sure to compare rates.

Upon settling in at your overnight accommodations, immediately plan your next step in the hunting process before you move on to the non-hunting activities.

This would be a good time to contact the flight service or guide to inform them that you have arrived and are ready to get started. If they are running ahead of schedule or there is less than desirable flying weather expected in the next few days don't be surprised if you are offered an opportunity to leave early. If this happens, jump on it; *never, ever* decline an opportunity to get to your hunt early as it may happen that you will not be able to leave on your scheduled date due to weather or some other tragic occurrence. Remember 9/11? That shut air operations down here for three days. Not even the bald eagles flew during that time without receiving an escort by an F-15!

Once you have a good feeling about your next step, relax, and enjoy the moment. Be sure to hobnob with the locals; don't pretend – they've probably already figured out that you are a visitor before you even open your mouth, but let them know that you are here to enjoy the legendary game animals that Alaska has to offer.

Everyone that comes up to hunt should have at least a couple of permanent friends in Alaska to help arrange stopovers and activities while you're here. Start looking for those friends. You might even run into someone looking for a hunting partner for a trophy moose hunting spot that they have picked out! The contacts you could establish over a cold beer or other beverage will be priceless; so from the time you step foot in Alaska for the first time to hunt, you should be planning your next visit.

We have excellent restaurants and pubs in Alaska, just ask the locals for directions to the better ones. You've probably already heard of "The Great Alaskan Bush Company", or if not, you will hear of it before you leave. Located in Anchorage, just a few miles from the airport, it's *not* a restaurant....I'll leave it at that. I hear there are some nice two-legged game animals in there, but you could never get a rug made out of one...

The buzz of the floatplanes around Lake Hood will definitely get your blood boiling. Lots of hunters leaving for hunts very similar to yours at all times of the day; now that's what I'm talkin' about! Lake Hood is the largest and busiest floatplane airport in the entire world, and is likely the starting place in route to further hunting destinations. Stop in at the Millennium Hotel or the West Coast International Hotel for a cold beverage just to watch the hunters and fishermen come and go during days with good flying weather. Those hotels are located on the shore of nearby Lake Hood and provide excellent viewing of the action on the lake. You'll definitely feel as if you've found a home away from home once you hear the buzz of the local aircraft.

Plan a short shopping spree to the local sporting goods stores. Pick up the last-minute items that you thought about during your flight into the state.

A more recent addition to Anchorage, Alaska is a huge sporting goods store called *"Sportsman's Warehouse"*. The entire store is staffed with knowledgeable, experienced hunters and fishermen who will provide the gear and advice that best suits your specific needs. I have found their prices to be lower than smaller stores, and their selection to be comprehensive. If I were afforded only one location to do my last-minute shopping prior to a hunt, this is where I would go. My book happens to be "built in" to the store, so you can always get an extra copy there!

If you will not be flying commercial airlines to the bush or a further destination in Alaska, you will need to purchase the fuel for your stove during one of these trips. Fuel canisters can be flown in by your bush pilot, once they have been properly declared, but *not* by a commercial airline.

I recently found this out the hard way, and had to purchase a new stove and fuel in Cordova, Alaska because the fuel canisters that they had available in Cordova did not match the high-speed-low drag 3.5oz. stove that I normally carry. This did not ruin my hunt, but did catch me off guard, so I won't allow this to happen again. It will ruin your hunt, however, if you allow yourself to be dropped at your hunting site without purchasing fuel for your stove. Freeze dried meals will wreck your digestive system if they are not properly hydrated prior to consumption, so this is **very important**.

Be sure that you do not buy more than you can store in your pack or bag that will be going into the field with you. The very last thing you want to do is show up at a flight service, packed up neat and lean, only to have an additional three or four plastic bags of "extras". This is very unsightly, and will immediately identify you as a novice to bush flying whether you are or not.

If you have not yet purchased a topographic map of your hunting area, now is the time to do it. *USGS Earth Science Information Center,* at 4230 University Drive in Anchorage will have the map that you are looking for, and is located just a ten minute taxi ride from the airport. In order to purchase a map of your hunting area, you must first know the exact location, which will be a lake, river, ridge or peak. Just explain to the air taxi or guide that you are interested in purchasing maps to the area, and they will likely tell you which one to purchase.

Folded properly, your map will fit into a quart-sized plastic sandwich bag, so lamination will not be necessary, but laminated maps will be more durable.

You're finally here. Take a deep breath and enjoy a lung-full of fresh Alaska air. You are welcome here, and you have just fulfilled an ambition that may have been years in the making.

Make sure your phone card is paid up, because you'll be calling all of your friends who could not make the commitment to coming with you. Of course, make the courtesy call to your loved ones and just for their sakes, tell them that you miss them and really can't wait to get back home.

Give me a call to say hello as well, then get out to the Alaska bush to make the memories that you will treasure for the rest of your days!

This could be your next stop if you will be flying into caribou country.

Those who fail to plan correctly may end up here!

IV.

Actions in the Hunting Area

*Weather must not be considered a barrier to hunting in the land
where weather is born. The use of aircraft can increase your odds
for success by providing access to hard-to-reach places.*

Access to Alaska

For the most part, we've only discussed how to go about hunting in Alaska by using a flight service to get you to the game animals. This is the preferred method, and the only way to access most of the state, but it needs to be said that there is some great hunting that can be done from the road systems of the state as well.

Most locals, especially near population centers, prefer to find spots close to home that do not require a flight service for accessibility. This is not the rule, just the trend. It stems in a great part from the lack of desire to put down $2,000 or more for a moose or a couple of caribou. Some pay for the solitude that a fly-in brings, and the added success rate associated with getting away from the "road hunters". A moose may yield 550 pounds of meat or so, but after you spend $2,000 for the meat, it comes to better than $3.50 per pound, and you can do that good at the grocery store; but not with a rifle in your hand. If hunting is your passion, then chances are you are willing to pay whatever is necessary to satisfy your desires.

If that same hunter can develop a certain "honey hole" within driving distance from home and can produce a moose, sheep, or a couple of caribou consistently in that location, then the only cost is the cost of gas and the foods that you will consume on the hunt! Now figure that out at a price per pound, and it comes to two families eating red meat for a year without purchasing it at a grocer at all.

I have yet to hunt sheep using an airplane for insertion and after three years in Alaska, and I have tagged a sheep on the two occasions that I've hunted. The sheep tags cost me *nada*, and all I have to show for it are two beautiful trophies and a higher than average cholesterol count because I eat too much red meat.

Now wouldn't you like to stumble upon a place like that in your own back yard? If you are a resident of Alaska, then it is entirely possible, and probable that you will be successful if you possess the skill and patience of a hunter and have *done your homework*. The homework is the most important factor because you cannot take a critter where they are not, regardless of how skillful and patient you are. If you follow my advice and always act upon planning your next hunt you will eventually run into a fellow like me who will invite you along.

You must hire a licensed guide or be the relative in the first degree of kin to an Alaska resident in order to hunt Dall sheep, mountain goats, and brown or grizzly bear in Alaska. If you are left to caribou, moose, and black bears, then so be it. I hope you recall how my buddy Dan came to take "Weyerhaeuser" home with him – he was friends with an Alaska resident...me! He now must look at a 74 ½" bull moose hanging in his living room when he wakes up to drink his coffee.

Is he planning on hiring a guide to hunt sheep or goats? Nope, he's content with two trophy bull caribou and a trophy bull moose; but he is talking about coming up for a black bear, and guess who knows where there are more than you can shake a stick at.... within driving distance of Anchorage!

Let me tell you a little secret. Once you have knowledge as to where the game animals are, you have greatly reduced the cost of your next hunt in Alaska. I'll explain: If you call from the "outside" and are looking for a flight service to put you on animals that they have knowledge of, then you will be paying for that knowledge. If you make that same phone call and just request an air taxi service to a particular lake, then that's all you will pay for is the cost of the airplane for the hours that you are in it. The going rate right now for an hour of flying is $250. You will be charged for the cost of flying out the meat and antlers, but not nearly as much as you would if you requested their knowledge of where the animals are. The bottom line is that you need to pay attention to where you are going and what you see on the way there. If you have the knowledge of a resident, then you will pay resident prices when you fly.

Enough about flying for now, let's talk about floating. Growing in popularity, float hunting has proven to be a very effective way to get away from the crowds to access the game. Whether you leave from a road, or you are dropped off by an air service, this form of hunting will increase your participation in the hunt because you will be setting the pace at which you travel a prearranged route on a river. This can be done to access all of the game that you have come here to hunt, as river habitats are home to moose, caribou, and black bears.

The authority on this subject is Larry Bartlett, whose book entitled; *"The Complete Guide to Float Hunting in Alaska"* is an outstanding reference for anyone considering entering the rivers of Alaska in pursuit of game. Do not attempt this feat until you have read the book, and even then it is not for everyone. Alaska Rivers run cold, fast, and in some instances, deep. You cannot successfully make the jump from the paddleboats at the city park to float hunting an Alaska river without nerves of steel and knowledge of what you will be up against.

Floating craft can be rented in Alaska if you choose to pursue this endeavor, so don't try to bring your own. Additionally, most flight services that offer moose or caribou hunts will probably offer a package deal for the use of their gear. Just ask. If you rent or borrow a floating craft, it is necessary that you inflate it and become accustomed to it prior to leaving for your hunting destination. A damaged craft will be dangerous to operate and it is the responsibility of the hunter to ensure that all equipment is operational before getting into the cold, fast running waters of Alaska.

Back to the use of a flight service:

This is by far the means of access that has historically proven to be the most successful; success being measured by the amount of game taken and by the least amount of other hunters that you will come across in a more remote destination. If it is extremely important to you not to see other hunters while on a hunting trip, then let your guide or flight service know that. You will never be guaranteed to be totally alone, even in the large expanses of the "Last Frontier", but a fly-in will provide the best chance at being alone with the critters.

The success associated with flying in does come with a price, as it is the most expensive means of accessing the state. It is not **un**affordable by any means, just keep in mind that the farther you fly, the more you will pay. Don't be surprised to be hunting not more than an hour from Anchorage, as some of the best hunting in the state is located within a close proximity of this population center.

Whether you fly, float, or drive to your hunting site, just remember to *hunt hard* once you get there!

Bob Doody and I embarking on a week-long mountain goat hunt in Southeast Alaska. Note the lack of gear "tonnage". You must learn to travel light and efficient to access the remote areas of The Great State.

Establishing a solid base camp should be your first priority upon arrival in your hunting area. Here, DeWayne Craig and I set up camp before the arrival of a drenching shower in sheep country.

Setting up Shelter

This is going to sound silly to you, but the first thing you will want to think about once you step foot in your hunting area is keeping your gear dry. Resist the temptation to take a quick peek over the ridge to see what the terrain looks like on the other side until you have established a camp. The weather in Alaska doesn't roll in from somewhere out west or north of where you are, it begins right above you, and can go from bright and beautiful to mean and nasty in a flash. Once you and your gear are wet, you be fighting to stay comfortable and that will require a great amount of effort; effort that is better spent in the pursuit of the game animals that you have come so far to "invite" home with you.

Start by selecting a bivouac site that is level in the spots that you will place your tent(s). This seems very natural, but in some areas that you will be hunting, it will be very challenging to find such an area. If the ground under your feet is moist when you arrive, then it will be drenched if and when rain comes, so take care that you have proper drainage of rainwater. The use of a ground tarp or "footprint" under your tent will extend the life of the flooring and add an extra vapor barrier that will keep unnecessary moisture from seeping from the ground into your tent.

Resist the temptation **not to** stake down your tent. Yes, you will have gear that may never leave your shelter for the duration of the hunt, but it is not heavy enough to keep the wind from wrecking your tent in your absence. Use stakes, then put boulders or deadfall on the top of the stakes to ensure that it will stay put. You won't realize how important this step is until your tent is flying like a kite across the lake or drainage that you are staying on.

Stake your tent for ventilation by using the guide wire points that are located on the outside. If your tent does not come with these points, then it is not sturdy enough to use in the weather that you may be experiencing. The added ventilation will be annoying at times, because you can feel wind blowing through your tent, but it will aid in removing unwanted moisture that will accumulate as a result of normal breathing at night. You will be much more comfortable dry and breezy than you will be if you are zipped up tight and moisture permeates everything that is inside of your tent.

At all cost, keep your sleeping bag dry, especially if you are hunting in cooler climate. At times my sleeping bag was the only dry piece of gear that I could maintain, and it made for a good, warm night's rest at the end of a miserably wet and cold hunting day. We both know that there are no miserable days hunting, just some more comfortable than others, right? The compression-stuff sacks that are designed to make your sleeping bag a smaller package are usually not water proof, so before you expose it to the elements, be absolutely sure that it is waterproof. I always put mine inside a plastic garbage bag for added insurance against moisture.

Try to put your tent near the tent of your hunting buddies to keep from unnecessary loud talking in your camp. At the end of the day, as you are preparing for sleep, you will rehash the day's events no matter how much you have discussed them earlier. The lower your voice, the lower the chance that you will alert the game animals to your presence. It is a very big mistake to think that just because you cannot be seen that your presence is not felt. If a squirrel gained access to your house you would probably figure it out in the same way that the critters will figure out that you have set up camp in their "backyard". With that thought in mind, do not consider starting a wood-burning fire unless you and everyone in your party are finished hunting. A fire will surely decrease your chances of success. The smoke will drift away only in the direction of the game animals, and with it will drift away the element of surprise.

I have included this chapter because it is very easy to get caught up in the moment, having just arrived at your hunting destination, and overlook the importance of properly establishing a site that will be your refuge from whatever nature may dish out. I am not pushing comfort-ability as more important than hunting hard to achieve your hunting successes; I am merely stressing that your energies should be focused at recovering your trophy from the field as opposed to recovering your control over the diminished condition of your gear and your motivation once you have allowed both to deteriorate.

Here are two pictures. One was taken at daybreak on the first day of a spring bear hunt. Notice the clear blue sky. The second was taken later in the day after the weather conditions had deteriorated substantially.

When we arrived back at camp after the day's hunt, Dewayne's tent was hanging on for dear life in a 50 mile per hour wind. We had to move it and all of his belongings to a more sheltered location. My tent took a beating, but stayed put because of its lower profile.

DeWayne makes breakfast at first light on a 0 degree morning.

It helps to think out a worse-case scenario with respect to wind and sudden weather. If you play it out before it happens, you will spend less time recovering your hunt from the abyss of deteriorated weather.

Remember, safety is your first priority, even on a "hunt hard" hunt. Stay dry, warm, well nourished, and well rested if your weather falls apart.

Later the same day with 50 mph winds and blowing snow. Note the absence of DeWayne's tent. Never underestimate Alaska's unforgiving climate.

During this hunt, we were tent-bound by driving snow for four days of a six-day hunt. We made the best of it by gaining about five pounds each, and by planning our sheep hunt, which would take place in August. (!)

Lin Turner travels 1000 miles by jet-boat down the Yukon River year-after-year to make his luck. Wouldn't it be nice to befriend someone like this during your trip?

Begin Making Your Luck

Once you have established your base camp and are comfortable with its durability, you may begin exploring the area adjacent to your camp. I say exploring in the sense that you should do a lot of looking and very little walking.

If you have flown in, then you may not hunt until after 3:00 a.m. on the following day, so don't be anxious to see the trophy of your dreams until you can legally hunt (him). There are some activities that you will want to start in order to improve your odds at drawing game animals close to you as opposed to having them move away from you.

First, mark your base camp with your GPS and locate it on your map. In addition, note the terrain in your general area and learn to identify it by terrain association from your map. This will be important in the days to come in case you cannot return to your camp in the daylight because it is necessary to remove the viscera from your downed trophy. I had this happen during a "new moon", leaving no light in the sky. It was as pitch-dark as I have ever seen it. This was before I hunted with a GPS so I relied on a sliver of light that reflected off the lake that we were camped on. This would have been well and good except for the fact that there was a very similar lake in another direction, and I mistook it for our base camp lake. I walked an extra two miles in the dark, on swampy tundra, when I should have made a beeline for our camp. This could easily have turned into a survival situation if we had inserted one or two additional factors like chill and precipitation, so I won't allow this to happen again. I hope that you take advantage of my mistakes and learn from them so that this will be the best money you've ever spent.

There is luck, or fortune, involved in every hunt that you will ever participate in. That even goes for the hunt on a fenced in game farm, because you're "lucky" that the owner-operator opened the business so you could hunt there. Of course anyone reading a book called "Hunting Hard – "would not be a person hunting on a fenced in game farm because that is "hardly hunting". My point being that there is luck involved no matter how skilled you may claim to be as a caller, stalker or shooter. That luck is influence-able, however by the interjection of skills that will allow you to at least claim that very little luck was involved because you were so *proactive* in your hunting efforts!

If you must wander the terrain prior to your hunting it, then be aware of natural travel routes and their relationship to the prevailing wind currents. Find a vantage point from which to *view* the surroundings to keep from *trouncing* the surroundings. The more your scent is spread, the less likely the game animals will want to wander into your area of influence. This is the reason that you have those binoculars and spotting scope. Use your optics to identify objects that are unidentifiable with the naked eye; if you rely heavily on your optics, then you will discover things that you would not normally see otherwise.

In caribou country there will be game trails that look similar to cattle trails. These have been used for hundreds of years, and your presence will have very little effect upon their sticking to their natural travel routes. In this case you would be seeking a position that will allow you to cover more than one travel route within your comfortable shooting range. Find a vantage point and stick to it until it produces or you see animals that you can approach undetected. Wandering aimlessly from hilltop to hilltop will only frustrate you and take you farther from camp. Remember, you must pack all edible meat back to a pick-up point, so don't wander too far unless that is what is absolutely necessary to get you near the critters.

I have a set of terms that I borrow from my Marine Corps days to describe the hunting area. They are the "area of influence", and the "area of interest". Picture a bull's-eye that contains only two circles; the inner circle is the area of influence, and you are located in the center of the bull's-eye. If you are standing at your camp or at your observation point, everything that you can see and hunt is under your influence. The area outside your area of influence in what interests you, because you cannot see it; hence the term "area of interest". Let's say that the area of interest extends as far out as you will be able to hunt given the time remaining in your hunt.

If you have just arrived at your camp and will begin to hunt at daylight tomorrow, for seven days, the area of interest seems endless. You may be able to take an animal as far as two miles away, and still pack him back to a departure point before the end of your hunt a week or so later. However, if you have only two days of hunting left, then you are limited as to how far you can travel and still fulfill all requirements of the hunt.

You must realistically "shrink" your area of influence with each passing day of your hunt. Do not irresponsibly take an animal that you cannot retrieve as your hunt comes to a close. No lines are drawn on the ground, so you must use your good judgment in this matter. I refer you back to the story of my Mulchatna caribou hunt. My archer buddy had traded in his bow for a rifle by the fourth day of the hunt, only to have an entire herd migrate through our camp on the next day. The moral of the story; be patient, use good judgment, and never give up hope.

Before and during the rutting period of Moose, which generally starts in the third week of September, *calling* moose can be as effective as calling wild turkeys. Moose respond to calling if their needs suit it, but they do so at a much more leisurely pace than you may be used to if you are a turkey hunter. It may take time to develop an area in order to move a big bull into the area; generally I would say three days. Developing an area means mixing your calling technique to *convincingly* sound like more than one moose. The key word being *convincingly.* This provides a mature bull with an opportunity to fight what he thinks is another bull and to mate with a cow. Wow! A bull can rarely pass that up!

To successfully call moose into range requires skill and practice. Listening to the sounds that a moose makes as he goes about his business is helpful in calling a moose in the future, so the residents of places that contain moose will always have the upper hand at mastering the sounds that are natural to moose.

If you would like to improve your chance for success by calling moose into range, then there is a resident authority here in Alaska that you will need to contact to learn the basics; Wayne Kubat, pilot, licensed guide, and the producer of two moose calling video tapes that are exceptional in their ability to instruct the hunter in the basics of calling moose. You can contact Wayne Kubat at:

Alaska Remote Guide Service

Wayne Kubat, Registered Guide/Outfitter

P.O. Box 874867

Wasilla, AK 99687

(907) 376-9568

I have yet to take a moose that I didn't call into range, and this year I took a bull moose with a bow from the ground at a distance of seven yards!

Say what you may about luck, fortune, or voodoo having some part in a hunt. I'll say, as long as I can influence my outcome in a positive way and still bring home the bacon, you can call me whatever you want – I'm calling myself *successful*.

*Luck had nothing to do with this bull moose finding the meat pole.
The late Buster Vanderpool, accompanied by Jerry and Clifford
Ivey, tend to their meat cache on a hunt near the Innoko River.*

Maintaining a Positive Mental Attitude

Hunting hard requires intense concentration and a high state of awareness as to what is happening in the area under your influence. Even the least physically- strenuous hunts can take a lot out of you. I usually arrive back at camp totally zapped of all energy after a full day of hunting, and sometimes find it hard to muster up the motivation even to cook something to eat! I can't explain the toll that is taken on the mental being, and really it is not necessary to have an explanation; just don't allow yourself to be overcome by long days of glassing and walking that have not ended in the taking of your desired trophy. If you have just staggered into camp after dark, totally worn out, imagine how you would feel it you were still in the bush with a downed bull moose on your hands and no one to help you with it? Of course, the actual answer to that is, "Elated!" but just try to get the picture that I'm trying to paint for you. I try to look at it like this... Every moment's passing is a moment closer to your desired result!

The next morning, when you wake to the constant patter of rain drops on your tent and the promise of a truly miserable experience looms at the next step of your foot; remember that the game animals you are pursuing do not stop their lives and head for the barn! They are still out there, not far from where they were yesterday; you will just have to give an extra amount of effort in order to find them. I've said this before and I'll say it again, "It rains *on* a hunt, it doesn't rain *out* a hunt". Keep your mind in the frame of excitement that you were in when you first arrived at the hunting site, because the only thing that has passed is time, and it is just a matter of time before you will be successful again.

I am a very spiritual man, with my own belief that we, as beings, are related on a spiritual level. With this in mind, at the start of each of my hunting days afield, I ask the following:

"If the Lord is willing, and my aim is true, I will take my desired trophy on this day; its flesh will nourish my body, and its memory will forever nourish my soul."

If on that day I am granted an opportunity to take the physical life of the kindred spirit that I am pursuing, then it was out of my hands that it should happen. If, on the other hand I am denied an opportunity, then it must be so that the time was not right. That's the way I look at it, and no one can take that away from me.

To give myself the best possible shot at this being my day of glory, I hunt with relentless fervor, so at the end of the day's events I am satisfied that I have done everything within my power to make that "kindred spirit" a memory that will "forever nourish my soul"!

Pushing the Limits...

Now that you've rescued yourself from a diminished positive mental attitude, remember that you are finally in Alaska; realizing dreams that many hunters never realize because they lack that special quality of commitment... Commitment to making their longings into reality. Count yourself with the successful having pulled off the trip in itself. You will be returning as a more enriched person for just having hunted "The Great Land", so make the best of it by giving your all to further that enrichment into the fulfilling of your ultimate dream...returning with meat and antlers to show for your efforts.

Pushing the Limits...of Endurance

You will now be reaching down inside for that extra measure of gumption to separate you from those that rely on mere chance. Finding ways to carry yourself over the near horizon, as the horizon is not getting much closer to you with time's passing alone.

Recall the story "Thirty-Hour Goat", when my buddy Dan and I were standing in deteriorating weather conditions pondering the outlook under crummy conditions. Our reaction was to plow on regardless to the task at hand; that being getting to the habitat of the mountain goats. It would have been much easier to settle into a camp and hope for the best, but why hope for the best when you can take measures to produce it!

I am not asking or suggesting that you endanger your life, or the life of your hunting buddies in any way. I am just asking that you propose, in the moment, which course of action will more likely lead to the fulfillment of your goal. If that means push farther, then push farther. If that means climb higher, then climb higher. If that means you must get out of your comfortable tent in the sleet, then get out and hunt in the sleet! Each hunt in Alaska whether you are accompanied by a posse of hunting buddies or not, is an individual hunt, and therefore an individual effort. Drive your efforts to produce the level of success that you want to achieve.

In the event that you return without meat or antlers to show for your efforts, you will have no one to question but yourself. The success of an Alaska hunting experience hinges on the individual effort of the hunter, and a relentless individual effort will produce game animals in the hand, in a land where there are game animals in many a bush.

Pushing the Limits...of Safety

<u>**Hypothermia**</u>

When you are charged by a brown or grizzly bear, there will be no doubt in your mind that you are being charged by a bear. Your eyes and your ears will tell you that a mistake has been made, and you may be about to pay for it. If you play your cards right, the bear may lose interest in you and move on.

There are many dangers lurking throughout the great state of Alaska, however none is more dangerous than the loss of core body heat referred to as "hypothermia". This silent killer will give no advance warning when a mistake has been made on your part, and once it takes a hold of you, it will not lose interest and move on.

Hypothermia is the loss of body heat at a rate faster than your body can replace it. You must avoid this occurrence as if your life depends upon it, because it does.

First your muscles will begin to shiver in an effort to manufacture more heat. Unless you have replaced the conditions that led to this symptom with more favorable conditions, your muscles will not be successful in containing the heat. There will be no pain as the cold replaces heat in the interior of your body. If you speak, your words may not come out as carefully as you may have thought they would. You may then feel very tired, and confused, because you're not thinking clearly. Fatigue will take over, and soon you will experience a strong desire to sleep. If you close your eyes as that feeling comes over you, then you may just have seen your last glimpse of life in the material world here on earth, and you may pass to the "happy hunting ground".

Frostbite

Do not confuse hypothermia with frostbite, which happens as the result of an exposure to extreme cold conditions. Frostbite happens externally, and usually occurs in the hands or feet because they are farthest from your core body heat. Frostbite will be accompanied by a painful stinging sensation as the flesh of that part of your body enters into the freezing process, damaging nerves and tissue permanently in the process. Unless you warm the body part that is suffering from the first stages of frostbite, you will lose that body part. All this drama, and hypothermia may never even have set in!

Prevention of Hypothermia and Frostbite

- Stay dry, under your clothing as well as the outside of your clothing.

- Dress in layers that can be removed in case you begin to perspire, or added in case you begin to chill.

- Have an extra set of dry clothes in your possession whenever possible.

- Eat regularly to provide your body with fuel to be converted to heat within your body.

- Drink water to keep hydrated. Muscles that are properly hydrated will operate efficiently, producing and holding heat effectively.

- Keep all skin from being exposed in extreme cold conditions.

- Limit the use of cotton in your garments. Cotton draws warmth away from your body.

- Shelter yourself from the wind whenever possible.

- Do not put yourself in a position where you may fall into water, unless you intend to be in that water.

Pushing the Limits...in Moving Water

The rivers that span Alaska are truly, sights to behold.

They take the lives of many Alaska residents each year. Do not for one second be deceived by what appears to be slow moving surface water. It has fooled even the most experienced water enthusiast into a false sense of security.   .

In most cases, what runs below the surface of a seemingly slow moving river is a raging torrent of icy cold water. If you are knocked off your feet while trying to cross, you will be swept downstream. Being swept downstream, in most places in the lower forty-eight, is a laughable matter that simply provides stories to be told to friends and family. If you are swept away by a river in Alaska, you will begin a very short fight for your life, and the image of your friends and family will be flashing before your eyes as the life escapes your cold body.

Whatever is on the other side is not worth your life, I can assure you, so think before you underestimate a river or stream while in Alaska.

In case you must:

When crossing any stream over ankle-deep, unfasten the straps of your backpack before beginning to cross. If you happen to slip, or be swept off your feet, landing in the water, you will not want to fight your pack as you are fighting to regain your footing.

Try to plant a trekking pole upriver and lean slightly into the pole with your knees and toes facing the current. If a strong current catches you in the back of the knees, it will sweep your feet from under you.

Pushing the Limits...in Steep Terrain

If you are struggling to keep your footing while traveling uphill, it will be doubly difficult when coming down.

It is extremely unnerving coming down a slope with any weight on your back. Try to side-step down, taking short steps, keeping your weight evenly distributed over the entire surface of your foot.

If that method is still making you sweat, then you need to be scooting along with your butt dragging the ground.

Plant your trekking pole, but use it only to keep your balance. It will slip from under you at the most inopportune time if you apply too much of your weight on it.

Friends, the obvious intent when coming to Alaska is to return, triumphant, to your family and friends. Do not take unnecessary chances with your life or the life of others in your quest for glory.

Alaska is as full of danger as it is full of beauty. Try to enjoy the beautiful aspects up close, while admiring the dangerous aspects from afar.

The varied terrain of Alaska will challenge your limits of endurance and patience. Maintain a positive mental attitude and document every aspect of your experience.

When you push the limits too far in Alaska:

<u>The elements can kill you.</u>

<u>Cold water can kill you.</u>

<u>A long fall can kill you.</u>

<u>Improper handling of a gun can kill you.</u>

...and then there are the bears!

This ice-cave, formed by running water through deep winter snow, was a barrier to a climb into sheep country. Safe travel and prudent decisions ensure that you will return to tell of your hunt.

Getting What You Came For

Shortly after making your commitment to come to Alaska, you should have put into your mind exactly what you would be coming to achieve. I am referring to the measure of success with reference to the specific type of game animal that you will seek.

Perceived trophy value is in the eye and memory of the possessor, and can be measured in inches of antler growth or in degree of fulfillment at having accomplished a feat. I, personally, am happier with the fact that I am looked upon as a hunter who gets his ram or bull year after year as opposed to seeking only record book representatives and thus being successful only on occasion. I am not inferring that there is a right and a wrong perception of success; I am merely suggesting that you decide for yourself, without external pressure or influence, what you will be happy with, and focus your efforts on giving it your best shot.

The largest white-tailed buck I ever shot came on a morning when I had slept beyond the ideal time to be in a position to take the buck at first light. I arrived at my hunting area late in the morning and happened to run into my trophy as he was leaving the area to bed for the day. This hunt, or should I say coincidental meeting, solidified my understanding that chance plays a great part in every hunt regardless of how educated we consider ourselves to be in the habitat and movement patterns or our quarry. Yet, in measure of trophy, where *eighths of inches* are concerned, this is my greatest accomplishment to date in respect to "measured" trophy value. Ironic that the buck that I worked the least for turned out to be the buck with the most *perceived value*. Visitors to my home remark at its splendor, and must wonder what a great hunter I am to have achieved such a nice trophy; but I know better.

Then there's the occasion where you climb and walk for nearly a week to have a barely-legal sheep grazing in your sights. As he stands unknowingly behind the crosshair of your scope you ponder whether he is deserving of your bullet; could there be a giant ram just over the next crest, or is he the best you can hope to achieve after such an arduous journey? I can assure you that my rifle will jerk in my hands nearly every time because to me, the commitment, work involved, and the mere chance that he and I have come together "in the moment" are enough to convince me that he will be treasured highly among my memories.

If you have never hunted Alaska, and this will be your first opportunity, then any game animal taken home with you should be considered a trophy. If you are selective, however, take the time to look over the game animals that you come into contact with before allowing the rifle to nudge your shoulder. An all-out trophy hunter, looking for nothing but a record book representative of a species should be prepared mentally to return from Alaska with satisfaction at merely "having hunted". I cannot justify that return; for my interests lie in a measure of success that is not so limiting.

Hunters of exceptional trophies are less successful hunt to hunt, but achieve maximum gratification from the acquisition of exceptional animals -- when they present themselves -- or when the hunter has privileged himself into a well guarded area with ample monetary compensation for the access to the area.

Chances are that the reader of this book sees things somewhat in the same manner that I see these matters, but the choice is yours. Make the decision before you reach the hunting site and stick to it with the same dogged determination that you chose when making the initial "firm commitment" to hunt this great land. Only then will you be guaranteed of a successful outcome.

Dirk Sterner, of Iowa, gets what he came for on our September caribou hunt in western Alaska. Scott Destival gets more than He bargained for.

The Shot!

This is the single moment in time that you have been waiting for. Relish it, for it will be fleeting; you will attempt to recapture it in your dreams, but it cannot be duplicated. In the months that follow your hunt, you'll try to remember the events that led to your taking the shot...

You'll remember that your pack made the perfect rest for the fore end of your rifle. You'll remember that there was a slight sting on the left side of your face from the chilled breeze that blew the swaying grass. The butt of the rifle tucked firmly into the pocket of your shoulder caused your cheek to rest naturally on the comb of the stock. The eye relief; perfect; no scope shadow; a crisp reticle stood cold against the heaving chest of the loping bull caribou. His beautiful white mane swayed ever so gently as his stride shortened. He stopped to look at his pursuing band of brothers, as if prompting them to hasten their pace. *There are many more miles to cover to our destination. This ground is so familiar, so traveled.* You'll remember his heavy, velvet-covered antlers, jutting high above his head and shoulders...

Your thumb nudges the safety switch to its lethal, forward position, followed gently by your fore finger resting naturally in the curve of the trigger. Countless times you have practiced these subtle movements, but never did they feel so surreal. You take one last drink of air, and then slowly allow it to escape until you reach that lucid place; where your intense focus on the reticle drives your mere existence. Without your knowledge or permission the rifle rocks your shoulder, but you do not feel the punishing blow, nor do you hear the explosion of powder; your focus; too intense...(to be continued)

Moments such as these are the reasons that I exist.

I was an excellent shot while a young Marine, so I was afforded an opportunity to become a Marine Scout-Sniper. Of course, there's much more to being a sniper than being a good shot, as there are many excellent shooters in the Corps, but very few are selected as Scout-Snipers. There are books that describe the characteristics of a sniper, so I won't dwell on the details involved. We will however, dissect the attributes of what leads to a well-placed shot. The fundamentals that apply to professional shooters also apply to the hunters of game animals.

The degree of accuracy necessary to take down a bull moose, which has a vital zone larger than two feet in diameter, may seem minimal; however, it's actually relative to what the individual shooter sees once the animal is standing behind the reticle of the scope. If you are aiming at merely the shoulder of the animal, then you may hit it in the shoulder, and all the time that you spent at the range in preparation for your hunt may have been in vain. If you aim at a particular patch of hair on the shoulder then you would be correctly applying the fundamentals of accurate shooting.

Before any hunt, I ensure the rifle that I am taking is performing at or near its capabilities. Consider your rifle a four-component instrument; those components being the rifle, the sighting system, the ammunition and the shooter. Weakness in any of the components will cause accuracy to suffer. An expensive scope placed atop a marginally accurate rifle will still produce a marginally accurate rifle, and vice-versa for any of the four components, as they all must be optimum to produce optimum result.

Accuracy is described in a term called *minutes of angle*. One *minute of angle* is equal to one inch at one hundred yards; two inches at two hundred yards; three inches at three hundred yards; and so on. A rifle that shoots a *minute of angle* is a very accurate rifle, and there are very few that will produce that kind of accuracy right out of the box; one that can is considered to be *inherently* accurate.

Inherent accuracy is very desirable when purchasing a new rifle, and brands and models that are known for their inherent accuracy should be sought out. As opposed to inherent accuracy, a rifle that is not particularly accurate can be improved upon by taking steps to reducing vibration between the stock and steel, and by experimenting with various ammunition loads. Seek the help of a professional gunsmith, or maybe you've got a buddy that does a great deal of accurate shooting and can provide some suggestions. The most important point here is to initially seek an inherently accurate rifle. My choice; *Remington model 700.*

Competition amongst companies that produce rifles is extremely stiff, which means that the over-the-counter rifles that are offered at Wal Mart are more than accurate enough to perform to the ability of most shooters. In addition, a rifle purchased at Wal Mart will always be less expensive than the same rifle purchased at a gun shop due to their massive purchasing power.

If you will be adding a scope to your rifle, you will get what you pay for. I own only *Leupold* scopes. The objective lens of the Vari-X III model is coated with a non-reflective coating, which allows light to pass through instead of reflecting off. This gives the shooter a bright, clear sight picture even in low-light conditions.

I prefer a thin duplex reticle as opposed to a thick duplex reticle. When my concentration takes over just before the shot, it is much more focused when the object of my focal efforts is thin. It is said that the thicker reticle stands out against the target in a more bold fashion, but I can't surrender my thin crosshairs.

In the case that you are not partial to *Leupold* as a brand, then seek the same qualities in another brand of scope.

When mounting your scope to your rifle, don't skimp on cheap rings and bases. They are very important to the integrity of the scope, and will be important to the rifle maintaining its accuracy after recoil and the abuse associated with travel and hunting activities. A single piece base is a bit heavier, but has more integrity than two-piece bases.

The ammunition that you shoot does not have to be hand loaded in order to be effective. I find that *Premium* ammunition made by *Federal Cartridge Company* will perform as well as hand loaded ammunition in most hunting situations. Loading your own will justify itself if you shoot often or are trying to achieve a desired effect, such as limiting the speed of your projectile to maximize the terminal performance of the projectile.

Hand-loading makes for an excellent hobby for the non-hunting seasons, and with experience will teach you more about improving the accuracy of your rifle, but it is not required in order to call yourself a serious hunter. Hunting with ammunition that you can find at any Wal Mart will guarantee that you will always be able to find ammunition that your rifle shoots well, as Wal Mart is as accessible in Alaska as it is in the lower forty-eight.

When choosing projectiles or cartridges to bring to Alaska, remember you will not be hunting thin-skinned animals here, so seek heavy loads that will penetrate, not explode upon impact.

Now add the shooter. Only a well-practiced and skilled shooter will be able to compliment the rifle, scope, and ammunition system that we have been discussing. It will help if you have a solid foundation of shooting skills and habits that a military background instills. If you are not a natural or military-made shooter, then you must learn and practice good habits. Go to the range in your town and ask the experienced shooters to give you pointers in the fundamentals. I caution you, however, that once you start asking for advice at a rifle range, you will be receiving more advice than you can process. Shooters love to talk; especially about their accomplishments and their infinite wisdom. Take only what you need and leave the rest, but take the part about *safety* and it being the most important aspect of handling a firearm.

You may ask; why would a fellow need a rifle that shoots that accurately when shooting at a bull moose, with a vital area the size of a keg of beer? The answer lies only with the desire of the shooter to shoot to the capabilities of the rifle system. If your best result at the range is a two-inch group at one hundred yards, and a four inch group at two hundred yards, then you are capable of two *minutes of angle*, and will likely hit the animal you are shooting at in Alaska. Be content with that if it is the best result that you can achieve, and expect to shoot less accurately than that when you are in the field. Field conditions, being less than the optimum conditions that you had on the range, will detract from the accuracy that you are accustomed to, so make sure that the accuracy you are accustomed to is the best that you can achieve.

Confidence in your abilities will lead to your hitting your moose or sheep where you intend to, so don't come to Alaska without the confidence and skill to make the most critical moment into a successful one.

If you will be using a licensed guide to aid you in getting within shooting distance of game, inform him honestly as to your capabilities and limitations, so that he will put you at the proper range to make the stopping shot. He will think more of you for being honest; less of you if you have crippled an animal with poor shooting skills and now he must find it.

Do not purchase a rifle for its recoil...That is, don't intentionally over-gun yourself in an effort to prepare for any situation that may arise in Alaska. If you are not accustomed to shooting accurately, possessing the disciplined traits of an accurate shooter, recoil will cause you to flinch at the most critical moment of the shot.

The current trend in rifle calibers is toward magnum calibers that carry the byproduct of punishing recoil. Be honest with yourself; if it is no fun to shoot, and you are turning your head to fire the rifle, its recoil is too heavy! If you are forced to have your barrel ported by a gunsmith, then you are over-gunned and should scale down. You probably purchased the heavy caliber for its performance characteristics; if you have it ported, you are now reducing its performance to gain comfort, so just choose a caliber that you can shoot comfortably.

I can personally shoot less than a minute of angle with both of my hunting rifles. The confidence that this fact gives me allows me to extend my shooting range in the field to beyond three hundred yards if it is necessary. I do not seek these shots, however, as the closer the distance of the shot the greater the margin of error that will be allowable and still achieve the desired result; taking an animal with one shot to the vital area.

Tips To Ensure That The Shot Hits Its Intended Mark

It is important when taking your shot in the field that you duplicate as many attributes of a shot taken at the rifle range. For instance, you ensure that there is something for the fore end of your rifle to rest upon at the range, so make sure that you provide a rest when in the field also. I like to use my day pack in both instances, as it will offer consistent vibration absorption at the range and in the bush. At all cost, make sure that the barrel of your rifle is not in contact with anything except the stock of your rifle whenever and wherever you shoot. Contact with your rifle barrel will cause your round to be off in the direction of the interference.

Clear your line of departure as well as your line of sight. If you are taking a shot through bushes or trees, ensure that your bullet will travel through without hitting an obstruction. You can clearly see the target, but can the bore of your rifle clearly see it? The high velocity of today's hunting rifle calibers do not allow for ricochet shots to be accurate. A small twig will cause a huge miss, even at close range!

Your trigger finger must be trained to perform consistently. There can be no rushed shot. A trigger should never be "pulled", or "jerked". Your rifle should fire as a result of slow, steady pressure applied to the trigger, and should surprise you by firing. Proper placement of the finger on the trigger is extremely important. You should be placing the pad of your index finger, just forward of the first crease opposite the knuckle, gently onto the trigger to begin the slow, steady squeeze. Too much finger into the trigger, for instance, the second pad of flesh, will cause your shot to pull at the "break" of the trigger. A rifle stock with too narrow a grip will cause too much finger to want to go to the trigger.

In order that your trigger will enhance the performance of your rifle, it can be adjusted by a gunsmith for resistance and travel. Resistance is measured in pounds; and it is not necessary to have less than four pounds of trigger pull for hunting situations. Over-the-counter triggers are purposely adjusted to be heavy at the factory. This is for safety concerns, to avoid the possibility of an accidental discharge or a premature discharge. (When I say, "break", I mean the crisp instant that the trigger releases the firing pin for forward travel.) There should be no noticeable creep, or travel, in the trigger before it breaks.

Take the time to learn your trigger by dry firing it over and over at the range, with your crosshairs on the target. Look for movement of the crosshair at the break of the trigger. The trigger's break, when adjusted to perform at its potential, should feel like the snap of a small glass rod!

Contrary to popular belief, it is not detrimental to your rifle to dry-fire it repeatedly in order to become accustomed to the break of the trigger. However, **always...always** check to ensure that the rifle is unloaded, by first visually inspecting, then physically inspecting the chamber prior to locking the bolt into the cocked position. Don't be the brainless idiot, declaring to the judge, "Sir, I thought it was unloaded..."

Rifle-stock technology has evolved in recent years to the point that it is difficult to find a rifle with a beautifully-grained wooden stock. What was proven adequate for a hundred years has quickly been replaced by composites and synthetics in the name of consistency and carefree maintenance.

You see, wooden stocks, when improperly dried, cured and sealed, will absorb moisture and warp when exposed to harsh conditions. This warping will affect the vibration at the instant of firing, which affects the strike of the round.

Composite stocks expand and contract less when exposed to the same conditions, and therefore have moved to the forefront of demand, replacing the elegance and appeal of wood.

With respect to the stock of the rifle, there are notable points to consider when choosing a new rifle. "Length of pull" is the distance from the butt pad of the rifle to face of the trigger. This is extremely important to the comforts of shooting, and is the major difference in rifles sold as "youth models". If the length of pull is too long, you will have trouble wrapping yourself around the rifle, and it will seem a struggle to manipulate the bolt. Too short a length of pull will cause you to swallow the rifle in your shoulder and cause your eye to naturally fall too close to the scope. This could prove problematic if your rifle is of the heavy recoil variety, as sooner or later you will be "bitten" by the scope when the rifle fires. Do not compromise where length of pull is concerned. Have it adjusted by a gunsmith should it be too long. If it is too short you are stuck, unless you replace the rifle with an after-market stock. I swear by *McMillan* stocks; the maker of the stock that I was accustomed to as a Marine Scout-Sniper. Therefore, they grace my rifle whenever it is necessary to purchase a better stock.

The width of the grip of the rifle is another consideration. The placement of your shooting hand will dictate how much of your trigger finger will lie naturally across the trigger. Heavy recoil rifles are fitted with thin grips, a little too thin for my liking. I suppose this is so you can "hold on" when firing it, but you will not successfully control the brute force of recoil by the mere grip of a hand. This is absorbed by the proper placement of the butt of the rifle within the pocket of the shoulder. A death-grip on the rifle will only cause loss of trigger control, and that is absolutely not recommended. I prefer a stock with a thicker grip. The bulk will promote a relaxed shooting hand, as the shooter will not subconsciously try to "grip" the grip.

To soften the blow of a heavy recoil rifle, have a *Pachmayr Decelerator Pad* installed to the butt of the rifle. The recoil will still be there, but it will come more in the form of a nudge than a blow.

The height of the scope is very important, and I mount my scope as low to the rifle as I can get it. You will be seeking to have your cheek firmly planted on the comb of your rifle stock. This is called *stock weld*. If your scope is mounted too high, your stock weld will be nonexistent, and you will struggle to maintain a perfect sight picture; without proper sight picture you cannot achieve a perfect shot time after time. Both of my rifles have a *cheek pad* mounted to the stock to raise my eye to naturally fall into the scope. Cheek pads are available through *Cabela's,* and I never attempt to shoot my rifle without one. You will be astounded when you find out what the addition of a cheek pad will do for your shooting. Make sure that it does not sit forward to the point that it interferes with the manipulation of your bolt, though.

Scope shadow is a disruption of a perfect sight picture caused when the eye is moved from the center of perfect alignment in the scope. Try this purposely to recognize it. A shadow will form in the side of your sight picture in the shape of a half-moon. If your shot is taken with scope shadow present in the scope, the strike of your bullet will be in the direction of the open end of the half moon shadow. If you learn to recognize this occurrence, you will condition yourself to eliminate it from your sight picture.

Eye relief is the distance from your pupil to the eyepiece lens of the scope. This is a fixed distance, and usually is optimal at three inches or so. You have perfect eye relief when the sight picture through your scope has a clear circle as an outer edge. If you are too far forward or back, the edges of the sight picture will be fuzzy. The length of pull, that we discussed earlier, will directly affect your ability to pick up perfect eye relief in a natural way. Do what you have to do to achieve a naturally perfect eye relief.

When firing at the rifle range, use a point of aim that is no more than twice the size of the group that you desire. At one hundred yards, I draw a black dot that is one and one half inches in diameter onto a piece of cardboard. That is the point that I am *aiming* at. My power setting on my scope is set at *seven*-power. This causes me to focus and concentrate intensely. A point of aim that is too large will require a lesser intensity of concentration and thus produce wider groups.

Point of impact, which is where the shots will penetrate the paper, may be slightly higher than my precise point of aim, as I usually desire that my group be located two inches above the center of the aiming point. Point of impact is negotiable, but point of aim is not; the center of the dot is perfectly quartered by my thin crosshair at the break of the trigger. Additionally, the focus of my eye is on the center of the reticle, not the target. In this way my eye's focus, and the center of the reticle with it, will seek to quarter the dot of my aiming point. If I focus on the aiming point, I will be chasing it with a floating crosshair, and produce a group that is larger in diameter.

The intake of air into your lungs should be at a relaxed, natural rate. Release half of a breath slowly until you reach a calm state, then hold. At that calm moment, which will effectively last for five to ten seconds, your heart rate will be diminished, allowing a steady crosshair to quarter the point of aim. Try to will the rifle to shoot. Your intense concentration should cause the shot to happen, not a pull or jerk of the trigger. In this manner the perfect quartering of the point of aim is not disturbed.

The same concentration practiced at the rifle range will become habit once you have conditioned yourself to require it before a shot is taken. This discipline will ensure deadly accurate shots in the bush.

Now, apply what you can of this information, which is not meant to address all aspects involved in the shot, just some of the more important aspects. Utilize the knowledge to make memories of your own, much like the shot described at the opening of this chapter.

The author demonstrates proper stock-weld in the sighting-in of his .270 caliber Remington "tack driver".

Things to ponder when your shot of a lifetime presents itself:

1. Safety – all aspects of it. There is no shot worth hurting yourself or someone else over.

2. Rest – is your rifle properly supported?

3. Stock Weld – is your eye "floating", or do you have a tight stock weld?

4. Sight Picture – you should be aiming at a particular spot. Are the outlines of your scope crisp? If so, begin concentrating on the reticle or front sight if you are shooting a non-scoped firearm.

5. Trigger Finger Placement – does your trigger finger lie naturally on the trigger? How about your grip on the rifle; it should not be too tight.

6. Concentration – do you feel the intense concentration of your reticle focus driving your trigger finger? ...BAAAAM!

Field Care of Your Trophy

(Continued)... Your deadly projectile has served its intended purpose; the bull caribou stumbles and expires quickly. Careful preparation and the chance meeting of your beings; these elements have allowed you to fell one of the most regal inhabitants of the Alaskan tundra.

You approach cautiously as the companions of the fallen monarch pause before moving on...*One has fallen, merely so that others may continue. Our safe ground seems more distant now. Urged by the calling, we continue our journey.*

You share a sense of accomplishment that has been passed down by hunters through thousands of years. However, you must surrender all feelings of *self*-accomplishment, for alone you did not accomplish this feat. You were accompanied by the souls of the hunters before you, and they have guided you to this ground in the same manner that the caribou were guided to this ground. The distant calling that first drew hunters to this great land, to stand on the very ground on which you stand, has compelled *you* to finally reach... *your* destination.

Take the time to offer thanks to those who have led you to this juncture; and display reverence for the gift of flesh and memory that lay before you.

Okay, snap out of it. This is where a number of challenges will begin. First you will need to get a large amount of meat cooled down and moved to a location convenient for transportation out of the bush. Secondly, you will be challenged to keep the meat cool and free of inhabitants. And lastly, you will need to take steps that will allow your memories to be passed down from generation to generation.

In the writing of this book I have tried to include only information that is not time sensitive; that is, information that will not change over time. However, I am not quoting from the *Alaska Hunting Regulations* for the year in which you will be hunting. As a matter of fact, I am not trying to quote the Alaska Hunting Regulations at all. It will be imperative, and I will mention this again, that you study and learn all regulations as they will apply to the specific game management unit, sub-unit and species that you will be hunting.

For now, as soon as you have the product of your labor before you, claim it. It is properly claimed as your possession once you have affixed the locking tag to a portion of the animal that you plan to recover, or once you have notched your paper tag with the date of taking. By law, this must be done before the animal is moved or processed in any way. The next step will be to skin and quarter your animal, but there are some specifics that pertain to this rather lengthy step:

- Explanation of evidence of sex: You must leave the scrotum and/or testicles, the penis, udder, teats, or the vaginal orifice attached to the meat or hide of an animal to prove its sex in hunts that are limited to one sex. Horns are evidence of sex in the case of Dall sheep.

- If there is a black bear lying at your feet, you may be recovering the hide and skull only. However, if it is before June 1st of the current year, you will be packing out the meat as well, *before* the hide and skull are packed out. Consult the regulations for the unit in which you are hunting for the details. It is a must that you do this before your hunt and have a firm grasp of what will be involved before you begin. Always leave evidence of sex attached to the bear hide! The claws must remain attached to *ALL* bear hides.

- Should you have a brown bear down; *and no longer breathing*, of course, it will be necessary to take only the hide and skull. The meat is optional on brown bears regardless of the time of year because of the fact that they are scavengers year-round. Again, always leave evidence of sex attached to the bear hide! The claws must remain attached to *all* bear hides.

- If you are hunting where there are antler restrictions or the taking of animals is limited to one sex, leave evidence of sex attached to the meat or hide. This is a good idea regardless of the unit or species that you hunt in for the sake of guaranteeing to a conservation officer that you have taken the correct sex of the species as indicated by your harvest tag. Horns are evidence of sex in the case of Dall sheep. In addition, all edible meat must be removed from the field, to the place it will be transported out of the bush or processed for storage, before any of the trophy qualities of your game animal, like antlers, horns, or cape. The horns, antlers or other trophy items may be transported simultaneously with the final load of meat.

- Wolf or wolverine; it is necessary to remove the hide only.

I cannot stress enough the importance of ensuring that you are following the regulations to the letter. Each unit may differ from the next, and ultimately, only you are responsible to the State of Alaska for adherence to the regulations.

For instance, there are game management units where meat of the leg quarters and ribs must remain attached to the bones for transport from the field. If you are unfortunate enough to be burdened with this chore, then you must strictly adhere to this regulation or you will be subject to having your entire animal confiscated! Oh yeah, and you will pay a hefty fine, also. Before I can begin to explain further, I must be sure that you are led in the right direction with regard to the regulations. Read them. Reread them; and ask questions!

You must understand the order of task importance in the removal of your animal from the field. I will attempt to explain each task as we progress, but this is not intended to be a manual for the processing of game in the field. I sincerely hope that someone in your hunting party has experience in the way of removing meat from an animal's carcass. If not, my explanations would be of very little value to you, as it would be nearly impossible to follow along in a reference book during the completion of this chore. You would simply have to "go for it" and hope for the best.

I will, however, give you the order in which I handle the tasks at hand, and pass along some of the trade tips that I have come across that may be of some help.   Each hunter in Alaska accomplishes these tasks in a different manner, and I have even heard of taking a *chainsaw* to the bush to aid in the quartering of a moose! My way is, simply put, *a method*. I won't be taking a chainsaw on a hunt, so here's the order in which I accomplish the removal of a downed game animal from the field:

*Note- "Eviscerate" means to "gut", or remove the organs and entrails.

> 1st – Claim the animal as yours through the proper use of issued tags. Affix the locking tags around the antlers, or through a small slit in the ear or other place in a part of the hide that will be recovered. Notch the correct date if you were issued a paper harvest ticket, to correspond to the date of take.
>
> 2nd – Mark the location of your downed animal with your GPS and with flagging tape or some recognizable item hung high so that it can be seen from a distance. This will eliminate excess travel in search of your animal the following day. The same goes for a pack that you put down to begin a stalk. – Flag it or you will spend a great deal of time searching for it later.
>
> 3rd – Remove the entrails and organs within a reasonable amount of time.
>
> 4th – Remove all edible meat from the remainder of the carcass.
>
> 5th – Put the meat to be harvested into game bags.

6th- Recover the trophy aspects of the animal from the remainder of the carcass and ready them for transportation.

7th – Transport all meat bags and trophy aspects from the field by hauling them to a departure point, where you will leave the bush.

8th – Give special attention to your cape, antlers or hide, to preserve them.

9th – Construct an adequately ventilated and covered holding area for the meat. Instructions later.

It is possible to remove the meat and cape from the carcass of the animal without removing the vitals and entrails, provided you have the time to start and complete the process within a reasonable time period. If you take the animal at a time approaching sunset, and you do not have the means available to recover it completely within the next two to three hours, then it will be necessary to eviscerate the animal, and ventilate it to limit spoilage and to promote the cooling process.

Never walk away from a downed animal because it has become too late or dark to eviscerate it. This has to be done, and I have done it alone, with no moonlight or a flashlight. My not being attentive enough to bring a flashlight caused this to be a miserable process, but I did get it done, and you must also get it done.

The Cause of Spoilage

The entrails contain harmful bacteria (E. choli) that will, combined with trapped heat and moisture, spoil a large amount of meat. You should remove these bacteria-carrying organs promptly after the animal dies.

Bacteria is present in living animals, but is kept in check by the elimination of waste product. When those products are no longer eliminated, the harmful bacteria begin to spread to surrounding tissue matter. This causes infection, or spoilage of meat.

The cooking process can kill bacteria, but you cannot kill the waste products that were produced by the bacteria, because they are *toxic*, but not *living*. These waste products are in some cases very harmful, and can cause sickness and even death in humans.

This is the reason that special care is taken to separate edible meat from bacteria-infected organs and entrails. The rapid cooling process slows down bacterial growth, but does not stop it all together; which is why meat spoils while sitting in your refrigerator. Cooling meat rapidly will only buy time, as time is the factor that must be overcome once the meat is properly cooled.

I will offer some situations that will provide you with a thought process on how to proceed once your animal is on the ground:

Situation 1 - Animal is downed in the morning, allowing ample time to eviscerate and remove meat, cape and antlers back to a departure point.

Situation 2 - Animal is downed in mid-afternoon, allowing time to remove meat from the animal, but not sufficient time to move everything to the departure point.

This is still a 'great deal' you have going on. Consider continuing into the night with the aid of a flashlight or lantern to get the job done. There will be plenty of time for rest and recovery on the following day. If you will not continue into the night, you must hang your meat bags to get them away from varmints and allow air circulation to promote cooling until you can haul them to the point of departure.

Situation 3 – Animal is felled in the evening.

If you can accomplish the entire process overnight with the aid of artificial light and help from your hunting buddies, then go for it. Be extra careful with knives using artificial light, because shadows will be cast over your work area. The danger of accidentally cutting yourself will be greater than with the full light of day. If the weather is cool, consider eviscerating, then opening the carcass up to cool it off. Leave lots of your scent in the area, like sweaty undergarments, to ward off predators and large omnivores (bears). Get a good night's rest and return first thing in the morning to do your boning, bagging, and hauling.

Dr. Steve Tierney helps me "operate" on this bull in order to begin the cooling process. Immediate and thorough cooling is crucial to keep precious game meat from spoiling

<u>Helpful Tips to Aid in Processing</u>

- Don't undertake this task by yourself unless you have to.

- Carefully saw through the pelvic bone to remove the bladder *intact*. This will keep it from being punctured and contaminating the edible meat.

- Have a clean tarp handy to lay the meat on as it is removed from the carcass. Spread the tarp over a thick bed of large branches to ensure proper airflow around the meat. The meat must be in a cooling process from the time you make your first knife cut until it goes into the freezer.

- If there are no flies, and the temperature is cool, allow the sun to dry (glaze) the meat before it is put into game bags. Later, flies will not be as attracted to dry meat bags as they would be if the bags were damp. Sprinkle the meat with ground pepper to make it less attractive to all bugs and scavengers.

- Clean and sanitize your knives often during the processing of edible meat. Use disinfectant wipes or soap and water.

- Keep excellent cuts of meat in separate bags than less desirable cuts, and mark the bags with tie-ties or cord near the knots in the bags. Don't overload the game bags.

- Use a separate knife for cuts around the anus or anywhere near fecal matter. If a separate knife is not available, clean and sanitize the dirty knife before continuing.

- Use the sharpening steel often to ensure that you are always using a sharp knife.

- If you lose sight of the blade of the knife while doing a cutting job, then account for your other hand's fingers before stroking with the knife. Most accidental cuts are made when you cannot see your fingers or the blade, keep them both in sight!

- Stop often and stand upright to allow your back muscles to relax. You will surely be carrying heavy loads later so don't tire or strain yourself unnecessarily.

- Always keep a vigilant eye out for bears and wolves, once they get a whiff of the meat smell that will be wafting through the air, they will come to investigate. Make a great deal of noise to alert any wandering critters of your presence, and keep a loaded firearm within reach, but at a state of safety.

- A large bear can eviscerate you much more efficiently than you are eviscerating your game animal. Take time to read the books of Larry Kaniut before you come to Alaska to learn just how efficient bears can be. *www.kaniut.com*

Transporting Your Meat and Trophy to the Departure Point

This will prove to be the most strenuous part of your entire hunt. When it's all over, you will look upon this aspect as one of the most rewarding, though. Not everyone can say that they have transported the edible meat of a moose or other large game animal overland on foot, so be proud to accomplish it. I know many a hunter that claims many a game animal, but has never carried one! Some are thankful for the advent of four-wheelers, and snow machines; I am thankful that my body is capable of doing my *heavy work*.

Your game bags full of meat will fit snugly to the pack frame, of your pack, pack bag removed. Just ensure that the game bags are lashed tightly to the frame in a criss-cross pattern that leaves no room for movement or "escape".

Now….travel!

Some good advice is warranted here. If you have far to travel, make the entire trip a series of short legs; that is, for a two mile pack-out, pack the entire animal halfway or a third of the way before proceeding to the departure point. The return trips will rejuvenate your energy level as you will have only an empty pack frame to carry. This is when you will have a snack, replenish your fluids, and restore blood sugar levels to normal.

When you unload the meat at intermittent stops, ensure that it is properly ventilated to continue the cooling process, and protected from the sun.

I now always wear knee braces for the packing of meat. You can act the *he-man* all you want; knee braces will save your knees from excessive punishment at the hands of heavy game bags and uneven ground. I'm sure there has not been a study done, but I'll go with the figure of ten years...that being how many additional seasons I will get out of my knees before they succumb to the stress of excessively heavy packs.

I have successfully packed moose and caribou for the long haul and for the series of short hauls. I have found that the short hauls do less damage to your mental and physical being.

Storage at the Departure Point

Bears will be attracted to your meat cache. If you store your meat cache in your camp, don't be surprised to find your camp ransacked on account of your meat cache is too close to your camp.

We will discuss two different methods of storing your meat at the departure point. I have used both, and there are advantages and disadvantages to both, depending on the situation that you have at the time. You decide which is right for your needs.

Meat Pole – A meat pole can be erected by leaning a sturdy tree that you have cut, or deadfall, at an angle against a sturdy tree.   Also, a sturdy limb can be erected between two trees. Whatever the method of meat pole you choose to erect, the key word is *sturdy*.   You will be hanging a great amount of weight from the tree or limb, and you will not want it to fall, especially while you are under it, adding the last bag.

Hang the meat so that it can be covered with a tarp to keep it dry during rainy periods, and out of direct sunlight.   Wind passing among the meat bags to cool them and dry them is essential, so don't crowd them together, or cover then totally.

Meat Rack – A meat rack can be constructed by cutting two-inch diameter limbs or deadfall.   Assemble the limbs to form a rack, off the ground, and in a shady area if there is one available. The length and width of the rack will depend on how many meat bags are to be placed upon it, as crowding must be avoided. String a tarp *above* the meat bags to allow air to flow among the bags. The tarp will protect the bags from sunlight and rain, but should not hinder the flow of air.

The bags must be turned at least once daily to promote even cooling.

You will be guarding the bags from infestation by flies that may lay eggs on the outer surface of the bags. If you notice fly eggs, remove them at once. The use of pepper, outlined earlier, will discourage the pests from landing on the bags to lay their eggs. If there is a hole in a bag, the flies will find it. Be careful not to poke holes in the bags. Holes should be mended or the bag should be replaced.

Care of the Cape

It is probable that your hunt will produce an animal worthy of being mounted by a taxidermist for future generations to admire.

This method of preserving your hunting memories allows others to behold and share the magic that you have experienced.

These possessions should not be looked upon as conquests, but as gifts of nature. I treasure my mounts highly, and with minimal attention I will be allowed to pass then to down for future generations to treasure and admire.

It is my opinion that "trophy" is measured in the eye and memory of those whom experienced the taking, and not in the taking of a tape measure to a trophy. You be the judge, and let no person diminish your opinion of your memory with "tape measure mentality".

Your goal is to provide your taxidermist with the best product to work with. Only if you have taken necessary steps to ensure a quality product can your taxidermist assure you of his delivery of a quality product. If the hair is falling out of your cape when you deliver it, the hair will not magically appear when you get it back some time later.

In removing the cape from the animal, care must be taken not to puncture the hide from the inside or at least to puncture it as few times as possible. All is not lost if the hide is lacerated, just be more careful as you proceed in order to limit the amount of lacerations to the hide.

For a head and shoulder mount, the cape should be removed approximately four inches to the rear of the shoulder. Provide the "artist" with as much "canvas" as you can in order to allow for a certain amount of shrinkage that will take place during the drying and tanning processes.

You will be attempting to avoid what taxidermists call "slipping" of the hide. "Slipping" refers to the hair slipping away from the hide when the hand is drawn over it. This very common detriment to the quality of your hide is caused by heat and moisture, which allow bacteria to devour the fragile bond between the hair and the follicle that contains it.

There are precautions and steps that can be taken to improve your chances of success in this endeavor. I will attempt to explain:

Cooling - The first of these is to get the hide cooled as soon as it is taken from the animal. The body heat that it may have retained must be allowed to escape. If there is a snow bank nearby, bury the hide in the snow bank to allow the cooling process to begin. In less than ideal conditions, just make the hide as cool as you can by allowing air to flow over it and shading it from the sun.

Do not submerge the hide in water to attempt to cool it. The added moisture will aid in the growth of bacteria, which is the primary cause of slipping of the hair.

Drying –Once the hide is cooled, the moisture must then be removed. This can be done with the aid of salt, or by air-drying the hide. First, however, all meat must be removed from the inside surface of the hide. This is called "fleshing" the hide. The object of fleshing is to remove as much the meat from the surface of the hide as possible, because it holds moisture. If allowed to remain attached for an extended period of time, the hair will surely slip from the surface opposite the un-fleshed hide.

Once the hide has been thoroughly fleshed, drying may begin by exposing the cool, fleshed hide to air currents. If salt is available, spread the hide and apply salt liberally to the fleshy side of the hide. The purpose of salt is to draw moisture out of the hide, leaving it dryer, and setting the hair. Additionally, the salt will inhibit the growth of bacteria. It is important to note that the moisture drawn out of the hide must be allowed to drain from the surface. This is easily done by placing the hide on the slope of a mound or hill.

Darin Brincks goes above and beyond for his hunting buddies by fleshing the cape of a downed bull moose. Proper care for your cape during the crucial hours following the skinning of the animal will make all the difference if you are having your trophy prepared by a taxidermist.

Do not expose the draining, drying hide to extended periods of sunlight. It is said to "burn" the hide, or glaze it. Glazing will inhibit the saturation of the acid solution that will later be introduced to the hide at the tannery. The acid solution will ensure that the hair will not slip, but only if the damage has not already been done.

Redistribute the salt, and reapply where it is needed, if additional salt is available. This drying period should continue until the hide is noticeably dry, and is no longer moist to the touch. This will take days, not hours. If you have ample time before you will depart the field, begin this process in earnest and aggressively attempt to end up with a dry cape or hide.

If time will not allow, then at least get the hide fleshed and air-dried as much as possible.

Your objective is to make the hide stable enough to undergo the travel that will be necessary to transport the hide or cape to your taxidermist.

Do not transport or store your cape in a plastic bag. This will inhibit drying by trapping moisture. When folded, the hide should be "skin-to-skin", not "hair-to-skin".

There is no "Hair Club for Capes". Hair lost will remain lost and will be unsightly on the finished product. Once the meat bags are put away, this must become your top priority.

Care of the Antlers or Horns

Even if the cape doesn't make it, you now have a set of antlers or horns that will last for many lifetimes. However, with the knowledge that you now have you will be very capable of transporting your cape or hide in a stable condition to your taxidermist.

There have been times when I did not attempt to cape an animal that I had taken for lack of resources, or the distance I would have to travel on foot was too great or too treacherous. In these cases, I leave the horns or antlers attached to the skull of the animal. All excess meat is removed from the head to keep the packing weight to a minimum.

One of my favorite methods of mounting a set of antlers is a method referred to as a "European Mount". This is a bleached skull with antlers or horns attached. It is an impressive looking mount, and has the additional benefit of providing a welcomed break from the high cost of a shoulder mount. Ask your taxidermist to perform this service for you if you are not pleased by the thought of boiling and bleaching the head of a game animal.

To remove the head from the animal, tilt the head forward on its nose. Make a cut at the base of the back of the head, just to the rear of the large knot of bone at the base of the skull. There is a large ball-joint that connects the skull to the spine. The ball of the joint has a tendon running through it that holds it to in place. That tendon will need to be severed to release the ball joint. Cut around the ball, once freed, and make cuts toward the lower mandible, or jaw bone. The rest of the process will be pretty self-evident, and no saw is needed for this process.

Removing the skull plate from an Alaskan animal is similar to removing the skull plate from a deer; just harder because the animal is larger, requiring more bone to be sawed through. This is the standard method for use in a shoulder mount, as the entire skull is not used; only the skull plate. You will need a sturdy folding saw for this procedure.

I do not advocate cutting the antlers off at the bases. Positioning them for a plaque mount, within any reasonable measure of accurate distance between the bases, becomes difficult once the antlers have been removed from the skull plate. Leave the skull plate attached if you will be mounting the antlers on a wall in any way.

If taken after a period of prolonged good weather, the antlers of a bull moose or caribou will look bleached, or extremely lightened by the sunlight. This aids tremendously in the spotting of animals, but is not as desirable in a wall mount, as it does not look natural. I find that the antlers look "washed" when this happens.

A method that I have of self-weathering the antlers is by mixing dirt with the blood of the animal, then smearing it over the antlers. When dried, this gives a natural brown color to the antlers; removing the washed appearance. When thoroughly dried, the dirt can be brushed away and the antlers will have a nice, natural look. This method of weathering sounds bizarre, but actually mimics the natural weathering process.

"Velvet", actually skin and hair, protect and help to carry nourishment to the antlers during their period of growth. After antler growth has reached its peak, the velvet dries and falls away, or is rubbed off by the moose or caribou. When the velvet first peels away, the antlers are a bright pink; colored by the blood seeping from the pores of the antler. The animals thrash brush and excavate dirt in displays of dominance, mixing the dirt with blood stain on the antlers. This effect produces the grand color of a beautiful set of antlers. By the introduction of blood and dirt, you have merely duplicated what has already happened, leaving out the bleaching by the sun.

If your animal is taken while in velvet, and your goal is to have it mounted in velvet, then you have a great task ahead of you.

First, you must avoid bumping, marring, or brushing the antlers against anything until the velvet has dried naturally. Any disturbance of the velvet will cause it to tear away from the antler. This is extremely hard to keep from doing considering you must move the antlers from the field, then move the antlers back to your hometown.

There is a process that taxidermists use that duplicates natural velvet. If you are committed to getting your antlers mounted in a velvet state; my suggestion is this process. It looks very natural, and many of your admirers will not know the difference unless you tell them otherwise.

If you have taken an animal in velvet and would like to remove the velvet easily, submerge the antlers in a lake or river. Tether it first and always soak it away from your source of water!

After a day of soaking, the velvet will peel off like the skin of a banana. Small pores will seep blood, so just smear some mud or dark dirt on the antlers to achieve the grand, weathered look.

The moral of this chapter is; do not compromise your material memories by being complacent with them prior to the completion of your hunt. I have experienced much regret at not having tried harder, on a few occasions, to better preserve my memories.

You have the benefit of my experience and mistakes in tending to these matters.

Through self-discipline and the application of the knowledge passed in these chapters of written words, you will possess memories that will be the envy of your friends and admirers.

V.

Departure

Depart Alaska with Reverence and Integrity

They say that all good things must come to an end. Fortunately for you this good thing never ends... as you are planning to make the long trip back to your home, you should already be contemplating and planning your next trip to "The Great Land."

In the event that you are not taking the trophy of your dreams home with you, as sometimes happens, keep in mind that you have merely lit the tender to this soon-to-be-raging fire. I have seen friends depart dejected at not having taken a game animal; they go through a smoldering process, and then the fire ignites again, at full flame. By the next season, they are calling me trying to arrange for another trip, having renewed the desire to continue the hunt where it may have left off.

The aging hunters, in the twilight of their hunting careers, find a way to return for just one more trip; again and again. The second-timers, drawn back by that unfinished hunt or maybe a crack at a different challenge, find a way to return again and again. Then there are those for whom the experience was much too overwhelming; they find a way to move to Alaska.

Regardless of the way in which you find yourself, when you depart Alaska, you must do so with reverence for the game animals that you have hunted or seen; the inhabitants that you have come in contact with; and the land in its natural state. At your hunting site, leave no trace of your visit except the footprints that you leave in the trails of the hunted. In your contact with the inhabitants of the villages and towns, leave the people with a respect and admiration for the honorable qualities of the hunters from the "Outside". You are a privileged guest, but you are paving the way of return for yourself and the hunters that will come after you. Ensure that the way is not paved with disrespect or deceit, but with honesty and respect.

Game biologists and law enforcement officers within a large community of professionals carefully think out regulations before passing them into law. These professionals are charged with protecting your rights as a hunter, and protecting the species' right to thrive in a land that was theirs long before man governed it. Travel to this great land with the intention of embracing these regulations. They are established to ensure that you and your grandchildren's children may enjoy the same privileges that you are privy to.

You begin with the permission of the State of Alaska by holding a non-resident license and harvest tag. You bring the gear that you will need for your endeavor, and the knowledge of the rules and regulations specific to the species you will hunt. At the beginning of your hunt you should have no questions concerning the legalities of downing your game animal, tagging it, moving it, or processing it for travel back to your home.

In the pursuit of meat and trophy, there are times when you will feel that certain regulations are a hindrance to what you have traveled so far to accomplish. Realize that it is not only the law that is broken when it is disregarded; you, as a person of integrity as well as passion, are breaking *yourself,* against the law. As the law is broken or bent, your integrity will stand broken or bent as well.

We have all experienced lapses of good judgment. At times our lapses are allowed to pass without serious consequence, but never without burden. Try harder at every opportunity to make the right choice. Each time you succeed, you have evolved into a more honorable being, capable of the discipline to handle any situation by doing the right thing.

One day you may sit to undertake a passing of information such as the one you are reading, don't bring with you the burden of truth at having achieved experiences through unsavory practice.

Remember, "trophy" is in the eye of the beholder.

How can someone convince me that this bull is not a trophy, when I had to take him at a distance of seven yards to keep him from kicking my butt?!

I had done a little too good of a job of calling him in, and he was convinced that he was coming to a fight. Clearly seeing me at a distance of fifteen yards, the bull continued his angry advance

My arrow struck him right above the brisket, from straight-on, and penetrated to the arteries above his heart. The most unbelievable part of this story is...he just tipped over once struck! I had already turned to run for my life.

The circumstance of the hunt dictates trophy value.

The Passing of Our Heritage

The thought of it is enough to make you cringe...after all of the scouting and hunting trips to your favorite "honey-hole", you arrive the day before the opening of season to find another hunter's camp in your favorite spot.   How can it be that something you've enjoyed exclusively for so long has been discovered?   And by another human being, no less; you're crushed at the possibility of not pursuing your quarry at your own pace.   Now, in order to be successful, you will be forced to compete with another of your kind – the relentless hunter who will stop at nothing in the quest for (your) "trophy".

Although we are guaranteed equal access to all lands that are public, imagine how horrible it will feel when this happens to you. It will happen to every hunter sooner or later because the population of this very limited planet doubles with each passing generation.   We spread flesh like a wildfire, consuming every patch of timber or wetland in order that we may live more comfortably and have all of our conveniences within a ten-minute drive.

As we increase our domain, we are limiting the habitat of our resources, which will in turn limit our access to, and the availability of those resources.　Unless you are a small-game hunter, satisfied with hunting within an hour's drive of your dwelling, you've no doubt competed for the game that you pursue.

In most western states in has come to the point where it is now necessary to apply for a lottery in order to acquire a hunting permit.　Our grandfathers would never have dreamed that in these same states, which once held unlimited resources, we must now compete even before we enter the field to compete.　As a result of misuse of the resource, this is what remains.　Hunting is passing from a heritage, enjoyed by all who cared to participate, to a sport of chance and skill in which we must first be lucky enough to acquire a permit, then best our opponent (the other hunter) in order to be successful.

Motives for hunting are varied, but for me, I desire to assert my position in the food chain, rather than gathering meat from a grocer.　Our "Hunter Educators" encourage parents or adults to take a child hunting in order that we may pass along the rich heritage and feeling of oneness with the environment.　The passing of this interest to our descendants will certainly prove important in keeping that heritage alive; however, there was a time when encouragement wasn't necessary.

In the not-so-distant past, a person's major source of encouragement may have come from the hunger pains in his stomach, coupled with the fact that the conveniences of shopping were not located as close as the corner of the block.　In that manner of thought, the only successful hunt was the one that put the squirrel in the pot.

Now, success is said to be measured in the level of fulfillment experienced during the hunt, regardless of whether an animal is taken to the table. This notion fits in perfectly with the fact that hunting is becoming more privileged through the limiting of our accessibility to the resource. Because we can no longer hunt when there is a necessity alone, we feel fortunate to be allowed the opportunity to participate, and therefore accept a fulfillment in merely having hunted! (?) There is no fault in this matter; just that we as hunters need to recognize that we are shifting our thinking to satisfy us with mere participation rather than the success associated with a full stockpot.

Are we to feel guilty when we return from the field feeling emptiness in our souls at not having taken our prize? If it is heritage that we pass along, then we should feel some shame at not having hunted hard enough or been stealthy enough to bring pride and protein to our families. I can assure you that to the last of the remaining subsistence hunters, returning from the ice-filled ocean without a whale does not bring any kind of pleasure at participation only. Participation simply does not feed the family or the village. Nothing but meat and blubber will satisfy the hunger in the stomach of the subsistence hunter, and that is their sole measure of success.

In our fervor to pass along the necessary knowledge to fulfill the heritage, we sometimes seem to keep guarded the most important facts. This came about when *competition for* the resource overcame our *privilege to* the resource. Just ask an accomplished sheep hunter where he goes to get his sheep. The answer will be vague at best, as if guarding his secret location will assure him a measure of success unattainable to the seeker. It is reasonable to believe this came about with the notion we refer to as "trophy".

"Trophy" is what separates those who selfishly withhold information from those truly willing to pass along knowledge. A hunter with trophy as a motive for hunting would abhor the thought that he gave away a location that may contain trophy members of a species, because the seeker may ultimately prove to be more "accomplished" if successful.(?)

On the other hand, the unselfish hunter, when passing along information, and ultimately the heritage, discloses all information; as success is not measured in inches of horn or antler, but by pounds of meat brought to the table, and by the gratification at having planted the seed of knowledge.

We are facing an increased competition, as hunters, in the pursuit of game. The rapid growth of our species within our finite environment will assure that there will someday be no sacred "honey-hole". Our *guaranteed* privilege is evolving into a *granted* privilege on a limited basis.

With this in mind, we must cherish our days spent afield in the pursuit of game. And we must pass along the hunting heritage that we have inherited with pure unselfishness, so that many may benefit from our knowledge and successes.

The Follow-up Shot

A little more than a year ago I sat down to document a terrific moose hunt that I had recently taken part in. Thinking that it sounded like a good story, I tried to peddle it to a few local magazines, but did not have any success. I finally found a magazine in the lower forty-eight to take it; they offered payment of a T-shirt and a couple of subscriptions.

Wow, I thought, it must really be difficult to make a living as a writer, as every outdoors magazine seems to be bulging at the seams with articles from "staff writers". Undaunted, I kept writing down accounts of hunts I had participated in since being in Alaska. An acquaintance, Larry Kaniut, offered that maybe I should assemble them into the form of a book. I figured it would take me twenty years or so before I would have enough stories to fill a book, so instead I began writing down everything that I knew about hunting since I had first come to Alaska. After a number of months, I had quite a collection of stories and ramblings, so I thought hard about the prospect of a book for Alaska's "beginners". The result is what you hold in your hand.

I am employed as an Executive Chef in the city of Anchorage; so fortunately for me I do not have to make a living with this book or any of my writings. I write because of the satisfaction I get when a friend reads one of my stories, and says, "Wow, that was a really good read." Additionally, I write because I want my grandchildren and great-grandchildren to someday, in a conversation, say to a friend, "You know, my grandfather used to write books."

So in a way, a book published is a legacy – a small piece of work that can never be undone. The knowledge that you take from this book also cannot be undone. Be kind enough to pass it along for the duration of its usefulness.

Every word that you hold in your hand came from my heart and from my mind. With the exception of the use of the "*Alaska Hunting Regulations*" edition *no. 43 July 1, 2002 – June 30, 2003*, I have used no other published information in the writing of this book. During the writing of this book I have been prompted to read the works of other authors concerning subjects that I have touched upon, but I declined, as my work was intended to be authentic in every way.

I understand now that there is at least one other book on the market for first time Alaska hunters, this being *"Hunt Alaska Now"*, by Dennis Confer. I urge you to seek this book, as well as any book about hunting in Alaska, as there is more useful information to be found than any one person can convey.

If upon completion of this book, you find that you have a longing for more information, that's because I have intended this work to be only a primer for more comprehensive works.

"Hunt Hard...In Alaska!" will be the first in a series of books that I will be writing, about hunting in Alaska. Please stay in touch by visiting my website, www.huntinghardinalaska.com, for upcoming releases and for products that will identify you as a hunter of "The Last Frontier".

Hunting the "Alaska Big Five":

Bear

Caribou

Dall Sheep

Moose

Mountain Goat

Appendix

Author-preferred airlines that service Alaska:
Alaska Airlines
www.alaskaairlines.com
1-800-252-7522

Northwest Airlines
www.nwa.com
1-800-225-2525

American Airlines
www.AA.com
1-800-433-7300

United Airlines
www.united.com
1-800-864-8331

Continental Airlines
www.continental.com
1-800-525-0280

Air Cargo Services out of Alaska:
Alaska Air Cargo
www.alaskaairlines.com
1-800-255-2752

Continental Air Cargo
1-800-525-0280

Airlines to destinations within Alaska:
Era Aviation
www.eraaviation.com
1-800-866-8394

Pen Air
1-800-448-4226

Air Cargo carriers within Alaska:
Northern Air Cargo
www.northernaircargo.com
1-800-727-2141

Era Aviation
www.eraaviation.com
1-907-243-3332

Pen Air Cargo
1-907-243-3322

Hotels and Inns:
All five of these Hotels/Inns are within close proximity of the airport and Lake Hood, and offer airport shuttle service.
Millennium Hotel Anchorage
www.millenniumhotels.com
1-907-243-2300

Westcoast International Inn
1-907-243-2233
Holiday Inn Express
1-907-248-8848

Marriott Courtyard
1-800-321-2211 or
1-907-245-0322
Best Western Barratt Inn
www.barrattinn.com
1-907-243-3131

Author-preferred local flight services and air taxi services:

I am only listing air services that I personally have had contact with, and would recommend. This is **not** meant to be a comprehensive list of the air services available to the Alaska hunter. I have listed them alphabetically.

Alaska Air Taxi
www.alaskaairtaxi.com
1-907-243-3944

Alaska West Air
www.alaskawestair.com
1-907-776-5147

Aniak Air Guides
www.aniakairguides.com
(Mar. 26-Oct. 1) 1-907-695-4540
(Oct.2-Mar.25)   1-907-495-9001

Jim Air
www.flyjimair.com
1-907-243-5161

Regal Air
www.alaska.net/~regalair
1-907-243-8535

Trailridge Air
www.trailridgeair.com
 1-907-248-0838

Willow Air
www.matnet.com/~wilair
1-907-495-6370

Gear Sources and Retailers, National:

Cabela's Outfitters
www.cabelas.com

Wal-Mart
(the one near your home)

Recreational Equipment, Inc.
www.rei.com

Frogg Toggs (raingear)
www.froggtoggs.com

Wiggy's (sleeping bag)
www.wiggys.com

Sportsman's Warehouse
www.sportsmanswarehouse.com

Gear Sources and Retailers, Anchorage:

Sportsman's Warehouse
8681 Old Seward Highway
Anchorage 907-644-1400

Mountain View Sports
3838 Old Seward Hwy.
Anchorage 907-563-8600

Wal-Mart (Mid-Town)
3101 A. Street
Anchorage 907-563-5900

Wal-Mart (South Anchorage)
8900 Old Seward Hwy.
Anchorage 907-344-5300

Alaska Department of Fish and Game

www.state.ak.us/adfg
P.O. Box 25526
Juneau, AK 99802-5526

Shipping of Antlers from Anchorage to Your Home:

Knight's Taxidermy
7329 Arctic Blvd.
Anchorage, AK 99518
907-345-5501

Hunter-Fisher Taxidermy
822 W. International Airport Rd.
Anchorage, AK 99518
907-561-1466

Additional Required Reading

Any and all books by Larry Kaniut. Purchase them at
www.kaniut.com
Alaska by James Michener
Hunt Alaska Now by Dennis Confer
Sheep Hunting in Alaska (Second Edition) by Tony Russ
A Complete Guide to Float Hunting Alaska (Second Edition) **and**
Caribou Hunting by Larry Bartlett   www.pristineventures.com
Bloodties by Ted Kerasote
A Sand County Almanac by Aldo Leopold
Beyond Fair Chase by Jim Posewitz

Index

DON'T FORGET YOUR HUNTING BUDDIES!

GIVE THE GIFT OF *Hunting Hard...In Alaska!*

Order online at www.huntinghardinalaska.com, or place your order here.

___ Yes, please send ___ copies of *Hunting Hard...In Alaska* for $**19.95** each.

___Yes, I would like to order **5** copies of *Hunting Hard...In Alaska* for the price of **4** copies! Just $**79.80**!

I am enclosing $**3.95** shipping and handling for the first book and $**1.95** for each additional book.

    ___ books X $19.95 = _____

    First Book S & H = $ 3.95

Additional S & H ___ X $ 1.95 = _____

Total Check or Money Order $ _____

Make Check Payable to *Hunting Hard...Alaska Adventures*.

Please allow two weeks for delivery.

Name   _____

Street Address _____

City or Township_____

Country   _____

Zip Code   _____

Telephone/E-mail _____

Mail to: Hunting Hard...   P. O. Box 233382 Anchorage, AK 99523-3382

Visit *www.huntinghardinalaska.com* for gear that will readily identify you as a hunter or future hunter of... "The Last Frontier"!